MW00711214

RIGHT UNDER YOUR FEET

You Can't Get Hurt With Dirt

Investing in Real Estate
in the Booming States
of Arizona, Florida, Nevada and Texas

By
Robert J. Davis

Copyright © 2004 by Robert J. Davis

All rights reserved. No part of this book shall be reproduced or transmitted in any form or by any means, electronic, mechanical, magnetic, photographic including photocopying, recording or by any information storage and retrieval system, without prior written permission of the publisher. No patent liability is assumed with respect to the use of the information contained herein. Although every precaution has been taken in the preparation of this book, the publisher and author assume no responsibility for errors or omissions. Neither is any liability assumed for damages resulting from the use of the information contained herein.

ISBN 0-7414-1987-4

Published by:

INFIN/ITY
PUBLISHING.COM

1094 New Dehaven Street, Suite 100
West Conshohocken, PA 19428-2713
Info@buybooksontheweb.com
www.buybooksontheweb.com
Toll-free (877) BUY BOOK
Local Phone (610) 941-9999
Fax (610) 941-9959

Printed in the United States of America

Printed on Recycled Paper

Published July 2004

Table of Contents

Dedication

To my wife, Janice. Having recently celebrated our 50th anniversary, and with six children and 14 grandchildren, you are still the same wonderful, caring and loving person I met in high school. Ever since that time when your classmates elected you Homecoming Queen, somebody is always telling me or other family members about your qualities. The ultimate compliment I have heard, hundreds of times, is "Bob, you've got the nicest wife!" They are right.

Acknowledgements

Dan Baldwin, my writer, the guy who takes my ideas, a few meetings and a lot of hand-written yellow pages and comes back with a book. This is our third book together and I just want to say thanks for all your talent, hard work, insight, your passion to see these projects through, and for your sense of humor along the way.

Carrie Martz, owner of the Martz Advertising Agency, has been invaluable for sharing her expertise on many facets of real estate. Several of her clients in Arizona and Nevada are owners of the finest real estate developments in these two booming states. Thanks for taking so much of your time and for giving me so many ideas that have worked so well.

A special thanks and well-deserved recognition must be given the thousands of top-notch, hard working and dedicated real estate brokers and agents I have worked with, learned from and been inspired by during the past thirty years. Your professionalism and trustworthiness in helping your clients buy and sell real estate is one of the chief reasons investors have done so remarkably well in this most fascinating and rewarding field of enterprise.

Introduction

If you've been blessed by God, fortune, nature, birth, perseverance, or just sheer luck and are living in Arizona, Florida, Nevada or Texas, count yourself among the luckiest people on the face of the Earth. I am not exaggerating one bit. These four states to my mind are the Earth's 21st Century garden spots. Judging by the number of excited people arriving from all over the U.S. and the world, millions of people agree with me. They're moving in to take part in an exciting financial and personal experience. They're arriving in droves to claim their fair share of the American Dream. Many of them will achieve that dream through owning a diversified portfolio of real estate, a portfolio providing income, cash flow, growth and appreciation in the value of that real estate.

People love living in those states. Arizona is my home now and I hear about that love all the time. People are constantly telling me how much they love the state, how happy they are, how the quality of their lives is so wonderful and so much better than before they made the move. My business and social activities also take me around the country. I get to visit Florida, Nevada and Texas a good bit and I hear the same comments from their residents. Often their attitude is, "Don't tell anybody how good we've got it here. We want to keep it all to ourselves." Sorry, friends, some secrets are just too good to keep. I put the quality of life, the opportunities for personal growth and financial wealth found in these four states up against those of any place on the planet.

Residents of Arizona, Florida, Nevada and Texas are truly the luckiest people in the world. And the best part is they can turn the good life into an even better life. I've seen it done. I've done it myself and I'd like to help you do it, too.

I've read letters to the editor in newspapers and magazines raving about how people love where they live.

Many of them brag about the wonderful differences between their old state and their new one. "State" often refers to much more than a mere physical location. Lots of people comment on their improved physical, emotional, and financial status, too. Living in one of these environments enhances the full human experience.

I've noticed a common thread among most of these folks. They weren't running *from* their old state. They were running *toward* a new and better one and that makes all the difference in the world. These people often left friends and family, secure homes and good jobs to move to one of these four states. And the key factor is, they really don't look upon the move as a hardship or involving a lot of sacrifice. Again, they were looking *forward* to *better* times. There's something about these four states that just attracts progressive, hard-working, and aggressive achievers.

Sure, you can find those who disagree. Arizona's too arid. Florida's too humid. Nevada's too glitzy. And Texas is just too big. These folks remind me of the people who inherit unexpected vast wealth and then complain about all the decisions they have to make spending it. Many of these types will never be satisfied regardless of their situation. To use an old saying, these folks really would look a gift horse in the mouth. They'll never find happiness because they never look for it nor do they really expect it. That's too bad because they are sitting on a gold mine of opportunity. (Throughout much of Arizona, that's literally true.)

One thing is certain and irrefutable – numbers don't lie. Arizona, Florida, Nevada and Texas are and will continue to be boom states. City, county and state populations keep growing. Fortunately, these four are also very big states and can accommodate such explosive growth. For example, the Phoenix/Mesa metro area where I live has just become the fifth largest in the country. Similar growth is being experienced in many other cities in Arizona and the other three states. I've arranged the states into three population categories to help emphasize my point.

Large states:	Florida and Texas
Middle size states:	Arizona
Small states:	Nevada

These four states have shown remarkable and sustained growth for long periods of time. Projections are for that trend to continue. In the cases of Arizona and Nevada that growth has been exponential during the latter half of the 20th century. The lush climate of Florida has attracted people since before the Spanish explorers arrived. Texas has been booming since GTT (Gone To Texas) started appearing on homes and farms after the devastation of the Civil War. Affordable air conditioning and a reliable water supply have made the Arizona and Nevada deserts bloom. This growth is no fluke. It is the product of vision and hard work.

Let's see how these four states stack up against the rest.

State-by-State Population, 1990 – 2000

State	1990	2000	% Change
1. Cali.	29,760,021	33,871,648	13.8
2. Texas	16,986,510	20,851,820	22.8
3. NY	17,990,455	18,976,457	5.5
4. Florida	12,937,926	15,982,378	23.5
5. Illinois	11,430,602	12,419,293	8.6
6. Penn.	11,881,643	12,281,054	3.4
7. Ohio	10,847,115	11,353,140	4.7
8. Michigan	9,295,297	9,938,444	6.9
9. NJ	7,730,188	8,414,350	8.9
10. Georgia	6,478,216	8,186,453	26.4

11. NC	6,628,637	8,049,313	21.4
12. Virginia	6,187,358	7,078,515	14.4
13. Mass.	6,016,425	6,349,097	5.5
14. Indiana	5,544,159	6,080,485	9.7
15. Wash.	4,866,692	5,894,121	21.1
16. Tenn.	4,877,185	5,689,283	16.7
17. Missouri	5,117,073	5,595,211	9.3
18. Wis.	4,891,769	5,363,675	9.6
19. Maryland	4,781,468	5,296,486	10.8
20. Arizona	3,665,228	5,130,632	40.0
21. Minnesota	4,375,099	4,919,479	12.4
22. Louisiana	4,219,973	4,468,976	5.9
23. Alabama	4,040,587	4,447,100	10.1
24. Colorado	3,294,394	4,301,261	30.6
25. Kentucky	3,685,296	4,041,769	9.7
26. SC	3,486,703	4,012,012	15.1
27. Oklahoma	3,145, 585	3,450,654	9.7
28. Oregon	2,842,321	3,421,399	20.4
29. Conn.	3,287,116	3,405,565	3.6
30. Iowa	2,776,755	2,926,324	5.4
31. Miss	2,573,216	2844, 658	10.5
32. Kansas	2,477,574	2,688,418	8.5
33. Arkansas	2,350,725	2,673,400	13.7
34. Utah	1,722,850	2,233,169	29.6
35. Nevada	1,201,833	1,998,257	66.3
36. NM	1,515,069	1,819,046	20.1
37. WV	1,793,477	1,808,344	0.8

38. Nebraska	1,578,385	1,711,263	8.4
39. Idaho	1,006,749	1,293,953	28.5
40. Maine	1,227,928	1,274,923	3.8
41. NH	1,109,252	1,235,786	11.4
42. Hawaii	1,108,229	1,211,537	9.3
43. RI	1,003,464	1,048,319	4.5
44. Montana	799,065	902,195	12.9
45. Delaware	666,168	783,600	17.6
46. S. Dakota	696,004	754,844	8.5
47. N. Dakota	638,800	642,200	0.5
48. Alaska	550,043	626,932	14.0
49. Vermont	562,758	608,827	8.2
50. Wash DC	606,900	572,059	-5.7
51. Wyoming	453,588	493,782	8.9

Don't think that because I'm so excited about these four states that I'm down on the others. The situation's not like that at all. All of our United States have many things to offer individuals, families and businesses. I just happen to think these four have more to offer than the rest and not just for the quality of life. These four states have by far the best potential for achieving wealth through buying, holding and selling real estate. Many people who say they'd love to move, nonetheless remain in their home states. Some have family ties. Others have jobs and job benefits they believe they can't duplicate. A few are just too intimidated by the prospect of change. I've encountered a lot of people who have just settled into their "comfort zone" and really don't want to make a move.

I know all about these feelings from deeply personal experience. My home state was Iowa, a wonderful place full of wonderful memories. My wife and I and our six children moved from Iowa City to Phoenix 33 years ago and we've never looked back. The contrasts are amazing. Our Iowa winters seemed to last five to six months and we were more than delighted to say goodbye to cold, harsh weather. When my Iowa friends are bundled up in coats, hats, mittens and snow boots, I'm often playing golf on one of my favorite, lush, green Arizona courses – in shorts and golf shoes!

One of the means we used to help us decide to move was the old, reliable "Benjamin Franklin" test. We took one of those legal size, 8 ½ x 11, yellow pads and drew a vertical line down the middle of a page. The left side was labeled Iowa and the right Arizona. Everything we loved about each state and how much that factor meant to us was put on the list. We took that test only one time. The list was lopsided in favor of Arizona at a ratio of six to one. That simple test pretty much made the decision for us.

Again, I'm not knocking Iowa or any other state. We've been back to visit friends and family numerous times over the years and we've thoroughly enjoyed every trip. Still, we never waver in our belief that our decision was the best one we've ever made. We are fortunate to live in one of the most exciting, beautiful and opportunity-filled states in the Union. Many of you can have equally joyous and fulfilling experiences by moving to any one of the "big four" states covered in this book. Those of you with the drive to succeed, the desire to dream big, and the will to make positive change in your life will come to understand exactly what I mean. You are the fortunate few indeed!

There's something else I've noticed. These four states have a large number of wealthy individuals, people who can easily afford second homes. Do you know where many of these folks buy their second homes? Often it's in the same state. Of course, many people have second homes in other states and even back in their home state. But it's telling to me that so many people with so many options choose to buy their second home in Arizona, Florida, Nevada and Texas. A lot of people eventually sell those second homes in their home states and look to a second home closer to the primary home. Here in Arizona that place is often in the wonderful forested country up in Flagstaff, Prescott, Sedona, or one of the many lovely communities in the mountains. People have discovered that "The Grand Canyon State" has eight to nine months of the finest weather you could ever ask for. People can have a home in the strikingly beautiful desert during the comfortable warm months. When the hot summer months become oppressive in Phoenix or Tucson, they move up to the tree-covered mountains to enjoy a beautiful cool summer with clear cool air and temperatures in the seventies. Although the environment is delightfully different, Florida, Nevada and Texas offer similar investment and retirement opportunities.

I intend to tout many of the various features of these four states, but this book isn't a travelogue. The "tours" I provide are targeted toward a very specific goal. That is to make you aware that Arizona, Florida, Nevada and Texas offer you the best, safest, quickest, and most lucrative ways to achieve whatever level of wealth you desire. The pathway is through buying, selling and reaping the incredible benefits of real estate. A friend of mine said, "The only way to make *real* money in life is to make money in your sleep." He meant that true financial wealth comes from having investments that continue earning money while you sleep, while you eat, while you play, and while you work to earn even more money. Real estate in one of the big four states can make that happen for you in a bigger, faster and better way than can be found in any other state. I'm convinced of that. I've dedicated my life to that principle.

The way to genuine wealth, a secure future, a better life, and the achievement of your life's dreams is right beneath your feet. If you're not standing on it right now, you can make a move and plant those feet on real opportunity faster and easier than you ever dreamed possible. These four states offer you, yes *you,* the finest real estate investment opportunities anywhere in the United States. That's a fact I'll prove to your satisfaction in the following pages.

Major changes have taken place since the year 2000. Many people appear to be rattled by the changes brought on during the first years of the 21st century: 9/11, war in Afghanistan, war in Iraq, "rumors of war" in other countries, political in-fighting, the unraveling of the stock and mutual funds markets, the scandals on or related to Wall Street, and a host of other crises. Well, when has the world ever been without turmoil? When has there ever been a century without war, financial crisis, or instability? Has there ever been a period in the history of the earth without crooked managers, dishonest business owners, unscrupulous accountants, or corrupt government officials? Whenever has the march of human progress ever been made without change?

There are lessons to be learned from history, especially financial history. Millions and millions of investors, many of the "mom 'n pop" investors, watched helplessly as their savings in stocks and mutual funds were pounded to death during the first three years of this century. Sure fortunes can and have been made in the stock market over time. But all that wealth can be wiped out in just a few bad years or in even less time when the market falls – as it inevitably does. Many saw their assets drop by 25 – 50 percent and some lost as much as 75 percent (or more!). This was especially true for those folks heavily invested in biotechnology or high technology stocks. Many of these failed or failing stocks and mutual funds had been the "darlings" of Wall Street and were highly touted by the "experts." In the end it was good old mom 'n pop who took it on their collective chins.

The primary focus of this book is to examine all of the advantages and the logic behind investing or repositioning most of your assets into diversified real estate holdings in one or more of the big four states. If you want to catch fish, you toss your bait where the fish are biting. If you want to earn real wealth in real estate, you move to and/or conduct business in the hot markets. No markets are hotter than

Arizona, Florida, Nevada and Texas. Why? There are three basic, overriding reasons: location, jobs and climate.

1. *Location.* All four states have great locations. Interstate highways, extensive rail lines, and regional/national/international airports, ports and ports of entry have linked all four to the rest of the United States and to the world. Commerce flows freely. Each state has an amazing variety of recreational opportunities and its own unique environment, landscapes, flora and fauna. These places are interesting, exciting and a lot of fun.

2. *Jobs.* Job growth in each of the four states has been nothing short of phenomenal during the last half of the 20th century and there are no signs of a slowdown. Better still, the growth has been across the board, from entry level positions to high-tech, high-paying employment at some of the most prestigious companies and organizations in the country. Are you an unskilled worker? A tradesman? A salesperson? An engineer? An educator? A corporate manager? A scientist? A doctor or dentist? An entrepreneur? Whatever your occupation or desired occupation, you can carve out your own niche in one of these states.

3. *Climate.* People have been coming out west for their health since Doc Holiday moved to Tombstone. Retirement communities have been springing up for decades and all four states have long been recognized as retirement havens. People move to these states because the environment is good for their physical health and mental well-being.

As I wrote earlier, if you live in one of the big four states, you are blessed. If you don't live in one, a blessing can be headed your way – if you'll head toward one of the big four. Don't you think it's time you earned your share of the American Dream? You can and you can start right now. And there's no better place to begin than chapter one of this book.

Of course, you don't have to live in any of these states to make quality real estate investments in Arizona, Florida, Nevada or Texas. However, it is much easier to get up to speed and remain current and informed about investment opportunities in the state where you reside. My reason for emphasizing a move is that these four states have the highest growth rates. Clearly something is going on in the big four and that something must be pretty good.

See you there.

Preface

Real Estate – The Only Real Investment

More people have become millionaires, multi-millionaires and even billionaires through real estate investment than through any other means. No ifs, ands or buts. Some conclusions are just not debatable and this is one of them. Today, real estate investment is the only smart place for the bulk of your investments. Period.

And when I say the bulk of your investments, I mean 75 percent or more of your total net worth. Depending on your needs and objectives, nothing compares to real estate for creating immediate income or growth and appreciation for the long term. Real estate allows you to tailor your investments for high income cash flow through first and second mortgages, state tax certificates, and discount mortgages. It is not uncommon to earn ten percent or more in the current market. For growth and appreciation you have unlimited opportunities to invest in a diversified portfolio. Some of the greatest home runs in real estate are raw land purchases in the explosive growth states of Arizona, Florida, Nevada and Texas.

Times have changed since 1999 when I wrote *Be Money Smart In Real Estate, Investments, and Insurance.* Events in the national and international economies, Wall Street, and in the big four states that are the subject of this book have dictated a major change in my investment strategy and I recommend that you follow my lead. I'll show you how. Whether you are a young person, single, married, middle-age, or a senior citizen, now is the time to reevaluate your investment procedures. Whether you want to acquire wealth or just protect it; whether you're saving for yourself or your family; whether you're building a financial empire or just securing your retirement years, realize that from this moment on it's time to invest your finances and your future in the broad spectrum of opportunity called real estate. The stock market and mutual funds have been attractive in the past, but for now they should not occupy a prominent place in your investment portfolio.

Regardless of your financial status, education, culture, age, sex, your goals, limitations, advantages or preferences, there are numerous real estate ventures in which you can participate right now. The more you invest and learn the ins and outs of the business, the more opportunities will present themselves to you. Riches can be yours if you want them, are willing to learn, and aren't afraid of working to become a successful real estate investor. What I'm saying isn't really new. Throughout history real estate has always been the pathway to wealth, power and success. That's certainly been proven again and again in the United States. The earliest explorers came to this continent looking for land, as did the immigrants, the settlers, and their descendents. Whether traveling the Santa Fe Trail, the Gila Trail, the Oregon Trail or any other of the famous roads west, those pioneers were traveling the path of real estate acquisition. They wanted land, farms, ranches, and towns with homes, neighborhoods, stores, factories, and schools.

I'm not saying there aren't other roads. Certainly entrepreneurs have invented new technologies, processes, and organizations and have created incredible wealth while doing so. Motion picture stars, recording artists, and professional athletes have become millionaires seemingly overnight. Other people have purchased stocks that have suddenly "gone through the roof," earning fantastic sums. A few lucky folks have even stumbled into the right place at the right time to become incredibly wealthy in virtually every field of endeavor you could name. It happens, but that's nothing compared to the track record of people investing in real estate. Over time, every other type of investment or money-making program pales in comparison to the vast number of people who have made vast sums of money investing in real estate. Nothing, and I do mean nothing, can compare. Nothing even comes close.

I have invested in the stock market and, in fact, I'm still active in it to a very, very limited degree. But times have changed and I have changed with them. The traumatic events related to the stock market crash of 2000, 2001, and 2002 were for me a wake up call. The wars in Afghanistan and Iraq and the general uneasiness of 2003 have made me take a different approach. Please don't get me wrong. I'm bullish on America, the economy, and the opportunities for great success now and in the long-term future. There's never been an economy like ours and I just don't see this engine running out of gas any time soon. This book is something like a road map you can use to come along for the ride if you so choose.

One of the primary reasons for this new direction is the chaos exhibited by the stock market during the first years of the new century. In all of my 40 years in business I've never seen anything like what's been happening and what continues to happen on Wall Street. You may be one of the 80 million Americans who lost 50 to 80 percent of your life savings in that horrible three-year stock market decline. If you experienced that meltdown with your money in stocks or mutual funds, you learned one of life's most valuable lessons – <u>never count on the stock market again as a safe place in which to invest your money.</u> Several million Americans previously retired have been forced to go back to work just to make ends meet. Millions more have had to postpone retirement. The risk of owning stocks and mutual funds is no longer a wise choice.

Bankruptcies reached an all time high in 2003. Officers and directors of some of the nation's most respected corporations have acted shamelessly and without any regard for their companies, employees, or stockholders. And they aren't the only bad apples in the Wall Street barrel. Untrustworthy stock market analysts and brokerage firms jumped all too eagerly on the bandwagon. Accountants and even some of the nation's leading accounting firms improperly stated earnings and performed countless irregular and illegal practices. Here's a short list of the kind of scandals that have hammered investors in recent years.

- In late 2001 energy giant Enron announced it was worth $1.2 billion less than it had been claiming. Debts and losses that had accumulated during the 1990s had been kept off the books, a move approved by its accounting firm, Arthur Andersen.

- Accounting firm Arthur Andersen was indicted for obstruction of justice by the Justice Department for destroying documents and e-mails related to its services to Enron.

- WorldCom filed bankruptcy in July, 2002 after being accused of falsifying balance sheets to hide expenses and inflate earnings, thus revealing accounting irregularities reaching $11 billion.

- American Airlines executives convinced rank and file employees to accept a loss of $1.8 billion in wage concessions while at the same time secretly protecting their own retirement benefits and compensation packages.

- MasterCard and Visa accepted a $3 billion dollar anti-trust settlement rather than face four million merchants seeking punitive damages in the $40 - $100 billion range.

- Martha Stewart, once a darling of Wall Street and the American public, was indicted for insider trading. She sold her shares of ImClone for $230,000 the day before the Food and Drug Administration rejected that company's application for a cancer drug. The price of the company's stock dropped like a rock, but only *after* Martha sold her shares.

- Samuel Waksal, who founded ImClone, pleaded guilty to insider trading.

- Telecom giant Global Crossing filed for bankruptcy, the fourth largest in U.S. history, leaving a legacy of misreported revenues and executives taking care of themselves at the expense of the shareholders and company employees. Guess which company served as auditor and financial counselor? You got it, Arthur Andersen.

- Adelphia, the nation's sixth largest cable television operator filed for bankruptcy after facing criminal and regulatory investigations into its corporate accounting.

- While admitting no guilt, Merrill Lynch paid a $100 million fine. Stock analysts were accused of promoting worthless stocks to investors.

- Xerox paid the largest fine ever imposed by the Securities and Exchange Commission.

- And look at mutual funds. In September, 2003 New York Attorney General Eliot Spitzer rocked the mutual fund world with allegations of trading abuses. Putnam, Janus, Strong, Bank of America, Prudential, Alger, Alliance, and Bank One have all been implicated in the biggest scandal in the mutual fund industry since The Great Depression.

Considering the depth and breadth of these scandals, and I doubt that we've heard the last of them, is it any wonder American investors are more than a little bit skittish? I mean, these companies and the men and women leading them were touted as among the best, most reliable and most profitable businesses and business people in the world. Unfortunately, when reality hit, it hit a lot of people in the pocketbook, bank account, retirement program, and plans for a safe and secure future. A lot of people are asking, "If this is the kind of performance I can expect, why the H___ should I put my money in stocks or mutual funds?" Why, indeed? Doesn't it make more sense to invest in something more substantial? Doesn't investment in a well-diversified portfolio of real estate sound more secure? Well, it does to me and that's exactly what I have been and will continue to practice.

If you have been investing in stocks or mutual funds prior to 2000, get out your records and take a look. You probably did well for a number of years, perhaps for decades, but look at what happened when you reach the year 2000. Compare the 1990s to the first years of the new century. Events during the past three years have eroded many, and, in some cases, all the profits of stock market and mutual fund investors. Many people have lost everything. If you've only been investing since 2000, you may have known only loss. Does this sound like a good way to create wealth?

Try this simple exercise. The next time you're outside, place your foot on the ground and give it a strong push. Then ask yourself which is firmer, the ground beneath your feet or a piece of paper. Sure, that's a bit of an exaggeration, but not as big a leap as you might think, especially in these days of corporate malfeasance, slipshod management, and care-lessness. Believe me, the investment action today really is beneath your feet – in real estate.

Personally, I'm no longer bullish on the stock market or mutual funds. I just don't think it's worth the risk of taking those kinds of chances again. Even if a stock looks particularly good, the odds are stacked against it. Remember, Enron was considered a sound company and a smart investment right up until it collapsed. It was a "hot" stock, so hot in fact that just about everyone involved got burned. Consider how many things can go wrong with such an investment: greedy officers and directors, unscrupulous accounting firms, increasing competition from global markets, and a host of other negative factors. One of the worst is class action lawsuits which seem to be more and more common. Legal expenses can suck up corporate profits like a sponge. They can even drive some companies out of business. It's a scary time to be invested in the stock market.

Real estate is much safer while offering a chance to earn serious money. First mortgages, trust deeds, and tax certificates provide much higher income at less risk than stocks, bonds, or mutual funds. Consider all the types of real estate options that are available to the investor:

- Raw land
- Raw land dedicated to commercial development
- Raw land dedicated to residential development
- Office buildings
- Shopping centers
- Mini-warehouses
- Industrial space
- Mobile home parks
- Rental homes
- Hotels and motels
- Vacation homes (2nd homes)
- Golf courses
- Resorts
- Parking lots
- Amusement parks
- Commercial property
- Mixed-use property
- Duplexes, four-plexes and apartments
- Apartment buildings
- Single family dwellings

And there are many other profitable options. In the pages that follow, I'll show you how to create wealth in real estate. How you define wealth and how far you take this new pathway is up to you. As we take our first bold steps into the new century, it's time to get back to the basics. It's time to realize and act upon one of the oldest realities in the world. The way to wealth lies right beneath your feet.

Chapter One

Real Estate
The Best, Safest, and Most Lucrative Place To Invest
Your Money

What a comeback for real estate! I've heard a good bit of talk like that recently. We've just been through a number of years when investment in stocks and mutual funds was perceived as the only way to build wealth. For many people the stock market was "it." All other avenues were considered second rate if they were considered at all. Unfortunately, many investors learned a very valuable, yet painful lesson at the end of the latest drop in the stock market. Isaac Newton said it many years ago. What goes up must come down.

In the real world, not some fanciful dream projected by financial analysts or corporate executives and their flacks, the only "it" is real estate. Seasoned real estate owners and investors just don't understand the attraction of the stock market. Why would anyone with common sense risk their earnings and investment dollars on such a rollercoaster when higher returns and greater stability are available through real estate?

According to *Personal Finance (May, 2003)* the Standard & Poor's 500 is projected to return as little as three percent a year in the coming decade. Real rates of return on investments could even fall into the negative column. In that issue the magazine's editor, Dr. Stephen Leeb, warns, "If you stake your portfolio on it, you will wind up with a fraction of what you had hoped for ten years from now." That's a pretty strong warning from a credible source. Growth in the area of three percent isn't really much growth at all, especially when you factor in inflation. In case anyone hasn't been reading newspapers and magazines, or listening to radio and television news, the article rather boldly states,

"The stock market dream is over." Leeb predicts that investors who blindly put their money in the S&P 500 will "lose their shirts." I could not agree more.

That's why so many people are looking to real estate. Of course, there never really was a comeback for real estate because those opportunities never went away. People just ignored the wealth beneath their feet to pursue a lot of pipe dreams over on Wall Street. Astute investors let the mob go its mindless way and continued to put their money in land, buildings, and properties. Have you noticed that during all the whining, moaning, and complaining about the mega-losses in the stock market during the past several years that you haven't heard a lot of complaints from the owners of real estate? That's because they don't really have them, or at least they don't have them on the scale of stock market investors. Most are quite happy with their returns. Their biggest battle at the moment is to refrain from saying, "I told you so."

When people gather at a dinner party or backyard barbeque, at some point the conversation turns to real estate. It's an inevitable topic. Stock prices have plummeted 35 - 50 percent or so from their highs of just a few years ago. In that same time real estate prices have surged upward 25 – 50 percent and higher! On top of that, mortgage rates have hit a 40-year low, boosting the home equity wealth of America's 74 million home owning households by some $1.8 *trillion.* That's an average of $24,300 per household, according to the National Association of Realtors.

Real estate is a safe haven for investors at virtually all income levels. It's something they can see, buy, and touch. It's real in a way printed or electronic numbers on a stock report can never be. Real estate means security in uncertain times and prosperity when the markets are rolling. After two decades of playing second fiddle to the stock market, real estate investments are now the favored place to invest 75 percent of a person's assets.

Here's how a breakdown of investments geared to safety, growth and security should look:

Real estate	75 Percent
Cash and bonds	15 Percent
Stocks (no mutual funds)	10 Percent

Of course, a smart investor will make allowances for his or her age and willingness to accept a certain level of risk. Overall, it's a pretty good breakdown of how your portfolio should be balanced.

Lou Dobbs, the 20-plus year anchor of CNN's top-rated Moneyline, made a profound statement in a recent interview on financial strategies. "I can't think of any part of the country in which I would not be invested in real estate. As Will Rogers said, they're not making any more of it." I respect Lou Dobbs and I respect his opinions. I advise you to do the same. He's right on the money.

The House Rules

Owning a home has been the single most effective way for most Americans to increase their net worth. Many individuals and families have begun very successful real estate careers with a first investment in a primary residence. That alone is a sound investment, but it also makes a powerful springboard into more lucrative ventures. In this country buying a home is affordable and easy. You can purchase a good home with just ten percent down. In some cases you can purchase a home with as little as five or even three percent down. You make the purchase and then sit back to allow the natural rise in value take place. Over time, real estate rarely depreciates in value and even depressed areas often bounce back to provide spectacular returns for the long-term investor.

Home ownership offers a number of advantages that set it apart and above other investments. For example, you earn a considerable tax break. You can deduct your interest payments and property taxes from your annual income tax and that's a substantial amount of money regardless of the size of your home. When you sell your home, you get to exclude up to $500,000 in capital gains from your taxable income if you are married and up to $250,000 if you are single. Capital gain is simply a financial gain resulting from the sale of a capital asset, such as a home.

I believe the single greatest advantage of owning your home is control. You call the shots. You make the decisions and you earn the profits from those decisions. You can't say that about stocks and mutual funds. In those investments your assets are in the control of managers and officers of the corporation, men and women who may or may not know their business, who may or may not be ethical, and men and women who may pick up and move to another company any time they wish. By no stretch of the imagination does that meet the definition of control.

"Leverage" means an amount of control over an investment or the capital to make an investment. It's an important concept and one I'll explore in greater detail in a later chapter. It works in all types of real estate investments, especially raw land. Leverage provides you with a means to earn huge returns on your investment money. The key is to control as much of the investment as you can with the least amount of down payment. For example, let's say John Doe wants to purchase 100 acres of land priced at $10,000 per acre for a total purchase price of $1,000,000. If he buys it outright, he puts down $1,000,000 and walks away with the property. But, if you use leveraging plus term payments and only make a ten percent down payment for that same property, you're out only $100,000 and you still walk away with the property.

If John sells the property for $11,000 per acre he makes a profit of ten percent. Not bad, but you will do better. Having bought using terms and leveraging you can sell the property for the same $11,000 per acre, *but you make 100 percent on the deal.* That's the power of leveraging.

This chart shows why leverage is such a powerful tool for the savvy investor.

Buying for cash

100 acres at $10,000 per acre = $1,000,000

Using leverage with terms
100 acres at $10,000 per acre

With 10 percent down payment=$100,000

If the land sells for $11,000 per acre, you make a gain of ten percent when making a cash purchase. When buying with leverage, you make a gain of 100 percent.

100 acres	$10,000 per acre, cash	$1,100,000	10% gain
100 acres	$10,000 per acre, 10% down	$1,100,000	100% gain

Bricks 'N Mortar

I learned a valuable lesson from a wise and experienced investor many years ago. His advice has helped me earn a lot of money over the years, build security for my family, and to weather the financial storms that have shaken our economy. "Invest all the money you can in 'bricks and mortar' and you'll make more money than you can ever imagine." He's been proven right time and time and time again. Paper (stocks and bonds) can quite literally be blown away by the winds of change, misfortune or an evolving economy. As the wolf learned from the last little piggy, you can't blow down bricks and mortar. They are substantial investments that stand the test of time.

What do I mean by "bricks and mortar?" I mean buildings and structures of all kinds, properties made to serve a purpose and last for years, decades and even longer. I'm speaking from a lifetime of experience. My first investment was in a motel and even now, after more than a quarter of a century, it's still paying gigantic returns.

Even a cursory examination of American history in the past century shows that most of the people who amassed genuine fortunes made that money through real estate. I think you'll find that many people who are credited with earning vast wealth in other areas began on a foundation of wealth built from real estate investment.

Considering the track record of the stock market during the first three years of the 21st Century, I think it's high time people started to reconsider investing in real estate. Even many financial advisors who tout the stock market have been advising their clients to lighten their portfolios of stocks and mutual funds. I am and always will be bullish on America and the American economy, but at the moment the stock market rollercoaster isn't the vehicle I'd choose to ride.

Real estate is an entirely different matter. The next time you drive through any part of any town, take a look at all the old buildings you pass. Many of them are in great shape and are still productive business and residential environments. They're still turning their investors a profit even after decades, often many decades, of use. I was in New York City not too long ago and I had the opportunity for a good look at a number of old, luxurious hotels and office buildings, some of them at or approaching 100 years in age. They were in excellent shape.

I thought about all the owners of those buildings and how generations of the same families could be earning significant returns on the initial investment. Imagine a lifetime, or several lifetimes earning money off a sound investment in bricks and mortar. Naturally, you're more likely to find these older properties in the long-settled communities in the East, yet even in the more recently settled areas of the West you can find excellent older properties for investment.

Good real estate buys are everywhere in this country. Over time even modest investments can earn huge returns. Additional benefits such as capital appreciation, income, and tax breaks sweeten the pot. I know investors who earn 20 to 30 percent on their real estate investment practically *every year.*

I've heard people bragging about making ten percent, 15 percent or even 20 percent in the stock market. Those times are long gone. Lou Dobbs, speaking in the previously mentioned interview, noted that the outlook for the financial markets is grim, that "We're not looking at double digit returns for the next several years. We're looking at high single digit returns, at best." That's fine, provided the stock market remains stable, which it can't. Even those high returns of earlier years pale compared to the returns real estate can bring over time. If you're investing not only for yourself but for future generations, those returns can be nothing short of phenomenal.

Here's the difference between investing in real estate compared to investing in stocks and/or mutual funds. When you own quality real estate, you will likely see outstanding returns every year. This is a certainty if you invest in 1st and 2nd mortgages (deeds of trust) or state tax certificates. When you invest in stocks and/or mutual funds, you may experience many good to excellent years, such as those roaring 1990s, but all those gains can be taken away in down years. The first three years of the 21st century proved that beyond a shadow of a doubt. When you suffer through several years of negative returns, you will need several years just to build back to where you're even. Most investors can't afford to wait for that to happen. The majority of investors since 2000 have less money now than they had four years ago.

I firmly believe that real estate investment is possible for almost everyone in America. Sure, many of you will have to start out small. So what? The important thing is to begin and to begin right away. Start off with an investment in a house, raw land, a small office building, a residential duplex, a small hotel or something in that range. You may even want to bring in a few partners to put something together quicker, to spread the risk, and to share expertise. As your experience, knowledge and income grows, branch out into more expansive and more lucrative ventures. You'll get the knack of it pretty quickly. And you'll be putting your money to work in the best, safest and most lucrative investments possible.

Chapter Two

Limit Your Investments in Stocks

Should You Invest in Stocks and/or Mutual Funds?

Basically...no.

Considering the current and likely future state of the stock market, I strongly advise against investing very much in stocks and absolutely nothing in mutual funds. Recent events uncovered by New York Attorney General Eliot Spitzer clearly show why you should not invest any money in the scandal-ridden mutual fund industry. There are two possible exceptions:

Its okay to place 5 – 15 percent of your net worth in stocks, not in mutual funds, *provided you are* **super knowledgeable** *in stocks, follow the stock market very closely, subscribe to Standard & Poor's Outlook or Valueline, and are prepared to suffer the consequences of losing some or all of your money.* Unless you can tick off a "yes" on each one of those items, you shouldn't even consider investing in the stock market.

Again, I have in the past been bullish on the stock market. Events in recent years have clearly indicated that at least for the foreseeable future, a bear approach is essential. When it comes to the stock market, it's time to hibernate. Why? Well, let's take a few moments to investigate the issues.

The stock market experienced three straight years of losses during the first three years of this new century. An event of that magnitude hasn't happened in more than six decades. You have to go back to The Great Depression to find a similar occurrence. Look at the numbers for the past three years.

	2000	2001	2002
Dow Jones Industrials	- 4.85	- 5.44	- 15.01
NASDAQ Composite	-39.29	- 21.05	- 31.53
Standard & Poor's	- 9.10	- 11.88	- 22.09
Wilshire 5000	- 10.93	- 10.89	- 20.85

That's incredible and I just don't see any reversal of that trend in the near future. These unbelievable losses in major indexes aren't flukes or blips or bumps in the road. *They're a pattern* and not a very attractive one for investors. Sure, we've seen some nice gains in 2003, but how long will they last? Investors are still reeling from the three previous years as they have less money now. Take another look at those numbers. It's easy to see how an investment could dissipate and even disappear in three years or less. This is especially true for the NASDAQ.

During 2002 the S&P 500 lost 23.4 percent, the NASDAQ lost 31.5 percent, and the average U.S. diversified mutual fund lost 22.6 percent. From the March 2000 peak to early October 2002, the S&P 500 Index lost roughly half its value. The NASDAQ Composite Index fared even worse, dropping more than 75 percent during the same period. Here's how that works with real numbers, using an arbitrary $300,000 as a base figure. If you had those funds invested in the S&P 500 during that same period your funds would at the end of year 2002 be worth only $150,000. If you'd invested them in the NASDAQ, you'd only have $75,000 left. How many investors can afford to take those kinds of hits?

"Playing the stock market" isn't a game. It's serious business with serious consequences and sometimes those consequences are devastating. It isn't like playing Monopoly. Millions of shocked individuals, families and investor groups have had their lives financially ruined during the past three years. Many of those poor (literally) folks will never get that money back. Many others will only rebuild a small portion of their savings.

18

You see the effects everywhere. Notice how many more retirees have re-entered the workforce during the last three years. How common is it to see a man in his seventies sacking groceries, greeting people at the local Wal-Mart, or flipping burgers down at the neighborhood fast food joint? A lot more than you did just a few years ago, right? This is the only way many people can afford to make ends meet after their stocks or mutual funds took a nose dive. Mortgage companies, apartment complex managers, utility companies, automobile companies, pharmacies and other businesses may sympathize, but they're in business to do business. They expect their bills to be paid whether you're in your prime earning years or past retirement. I've met people who believed they had built a secure future who now can't make house payments or who can't afford those wonderful vacations they've always dreamed about.

A lot of fortunes and futures crashed with Enron, Worldcom, Tyco, Aldelphia Communications, Global Crossing and too many others. For many, there's just not enough time to recover. Sadly, these days there's a lot of tarnish on those golden years.

Take Off the Rose-Colored Glasses

That's not a rosy tint. It's red ink! Whether you've been invested in the stock market for years, several years, or are just now thinking about it, reconsider your options. Investing in stocks and/or mutual funds is very risky at best. I know lots of people who didn't believe the recent plummet in the market possible. They grew complacent during the heavy growth years of the 1990s. Many of them were new to the market and had never experienced anything other than continuing increases in value. They didn't realize the fundamental rule that a bull market will eventually become a bear market. It's an undeniable fact of life.

Many of these people were in shock when seemingly overnight their fortunes disappeared. I encountered a lot of

19

people who had the famous "thousand yard stare" of the combat soldier who had seen too much battle. That same glassy-eyed look was on the face of millions of stock and mutual fund investors during the first three years of the 21st century. Too many investors have lost focus. They think the current trend is a mere "blip" on the screen or just a temporary disruption. Open your eyes, please. A sensible person just can't overlook the devastation that the last three years have brought about. You can feel it in your pocketbook, in your plans for the future, in your hopes and in your dreams.

Diversify Your Investments, Solidify Your Future

Although I have more than four decades in business, I'm just like everybody else when it comes to the stock market. I don't know what is going to happen next. No one does. How do you address an unknown future? I wrote *Be Money Smart in Real Estate, Investments and Insurance* in 1999. I would like to share some of my insights from that book with you to answer that question.

"I don't believe in putting all your eggs in one basket regardless of how attractive that basket may be. Realize that a severe downturn in the stock market could be devastating to your financial future. If I can make you aware of the risk, I feel that I have done my job. If you say, "I don't care" and decide to invest all your money in stocks and mutual funds, well at least you have been warned. Who knows? Maybe you will be one of the lucky ones who beat the odds. Or you might take a hit that could take you five to ten years or longer to get back where you were. It's happened before.

"I strongly believe in owning stocks and mutual funds as part of a total investment portfolio. The operative word is "part." I also believe strongly in real estate investments: raw land, hotels, shopping

centers, golf courses, office buildings, apartments and so on. I also am a firm believer in using your own creativity and drive to open, build and thrive in your own business.

"As of this date, millions of investors have realized 15 – 20 percent and higher gains on their money almost every year since the October, 1987 'massacre.' It's been a wild, wonderful ride for a lot of investors, so much so that many have allowed wild speculation and greed overtake logic. People act as if a 15 – 20 percent or higher gain every year is a sure thing, almost a right. From first-hand experience, I know that many people believe that the only way to make real money is in the stock market. Many have invested 100 percent of their money in stocks and mutual funds. Even experienced people in their 50s or older and who should know better are buying into this nonsense. Total greed has taken over the mindset of many investors. Does anyone remember the stock market crash of 1929?

"The American Indians say that life is like a wheel. Everything keeps coming around again and again. I'm not predicting another worldwide crash like 1929, but I do know that every up is followed by a down. That is universal law and it applies to basketballs, airplanes, life itself, and, yes, the stock market."

I have invested my entire career advising individuals, families, corporations and organizations on a multitude of financial matters. Without bragging, I have a pretty good track record. Yet, during the nineties I could not convince most people to reduce the percentage of assets in stocks or mutual funds. Not only were they investing 100 percent of their money in the market, many were borrowing money on "margin accounts." They were on an upward moving rollercoaster and refused to see an approaching downside.

They just wouldn't listen to the voice of experience. The three years of consecutive downturns were devastating.

As I noted, I am not anti-stock market. I'm just very careful about where I put my money. I have about five percent of my total net worth in stocks. I do not own a single mutual fund and never will again. There are many excellent reasons for my careful and conservative approach to the stock market. Keep in mind that I've played this "game" for decades. I've studied it from every angle and I make a point to be on top of things 24/7. I'm the exception, not the rule. I believe, as do many others, that the stock market just isn't the place for most people to be - now and in the foreseeable future.

What is a Stock?

Many people invest in stocks without ever seriously dissecting those stocks or even giving the serious necessary thought prior to making that investment. They generally invest in well-known names or follow tips from friends, relatives and associates. I'm always amazed at how willing some people are to bet hard-earned money on a totally unknown quantity. "My cousin says this thing is a 'can't miss' investment" or "I got this straight from the horses mouth" aren't very good investment strategies. I would like to look at stocks from a different perspective.

First, a stock is just a piece of a company, a piece that you want to own. You put up your money for a sheet of paper, called a stock certificate, that represents your ownership. There are two major drawbacks to this arrangement:

1. Investors don't really have much security,

2. Investors have little or no real say in running their company.

Sure, once a year you get to sign a proxy, but that's meaningless in terms of real power or real say-so in the day-to-day running of the company. You're just one of many investors, a small voice in a very large crowd, not a manager.

Of course you'll have the "opportunity" to enhance the profit picture for officers and selected employees of the company. When you sign that proxy you'll most likely be voting on increased stock options and other benefits for the folks in upper management. This is probably the main reason I lack confidence in the stock market. It's too easy for these managers to feather their own nests at the expense of the shareholders. For example, the officers probably had a wonderful and lucrative stock option plan in effect before 2000. Someday this plan would make them rich provided the company performed well and the stock prices continued to climb.

This happened time and time again during the bull markets of the 1980s and 1990s. Thousands of officers and upper-level employees made out like bandits. Why not? Many of them acted like bandits, didn't they? Motivated by insider information they cashed in their chips while millions of stockholders kept pouring their personal wealth into the stock market. The stockholders are partly to blame, also. Blinded by dreams of vast wealth and buoyed by investor euphoria, especially for the high-technology and biotech industries, they kept pouring money into the system. They thought they had at last found the answer to earning wealth.

Unfortunately, things didn't turn out that way. Many if not most of these companies had no legitimate reason for their high stock prices. Many were bleeding red ink even while they touted their own success, growth and strong future. I was continually amazed at how prices would rise for companies that were not making a profit. A lot of them weren't even close to making a profit. But prices kept on soaring because there were always more buyers than sellers. Logic flew, or was tossed, out the window and people just kept trading personal checks for stock certificates.

It was good for a while, but then everything became a game of smoke and mirrors, anything to keep the investors and the public from discovering what was really going on. Of course, the investors played along too. They didn't want to miss out on bragging to their friends about all the money they'd just made. I'm sure that felt great – for a while. Then, beginning in 2000, companies listed in the stock market dropped 50, 70 and even 95 percent from their previous high points. Many companies went completely under. The annual reports and proxy statements were written in a manner that disguised what was really going on. Investors, some of them self-deluded and others a bit too trusting, bought the corporate line and kept pouring in the money.

There was always something optimistic in those reports. But here's the kicker. Those investors kept approving brand new stock option programs for the officers, programs that reflected the changes current in the economy. Those officers just couldn't lose unless the company never recovered and went under. If, as in many cases, the company bounced back, the increases in stock values made those officers wealthy. For example, they may have had options to buy a stock at $40 a share in the 1990s. Prices started dropping in 2000 so they never exercised those options. Instead, they arranged for the company to send out a new proxy to the investors. The proxy included a clause allowing the officers to buy stock at just $10 a share. Naturally, this boon was denied to the rank-and-file investor. What does this mean? Well, you bought your stock at $40 a share. Its value declined to $10 a share, so the stock lost 75 percent of its value. The average stockholders got clobbered while the officers cleaned up at the new, lower prices.

Develop A Wiser Investment Plan

It's time for a little financial self-evaluation. After three years of declines in the stock market, what is your situation? Get out all your financial records to see what you started with and what you have left. Were the purchases worth the effort? Did hanging in there pay off the way you expected? Even if you invested heavily in stocks and/or mutual funds in the 1990s, or even before, pay close attention to what happened between 2000 and 2002. In many cases people lost all or most of their gains made during the nineties. I hope you weren't among them, but the odds are against that hope.

Why did all those stocks and mutual funds take such a nose dive? We've seen a few primary reasons already. There are a few more. Many CEOs and/or accountants were self-serving, greedy and untrustworthy. They never really gave a serious thought to fiscal responsibility, serving the customer, building a sound company, or protecting their investors. Their goal was simply to increase their personal share of the corporate pie and to gobble up as much profit as possible.

Many companies filed for bankruptcy. Scandals in accounting procedures were rampant. Some of the best-known, most-respected companies listed on the New York Stock Exchange were fined for making false or misleading reports. News coverage moved stories from the financial page to the front page as scandal after scandal rocked the nation's faith in some of its most powerful business institutions.

The nation's lawyers got in on the bandwagon, too. They just couldn't wait to get rich by filing class action lawsuits. That alone can force a company into filing for bankruptcy or to even go under. Do you really think all that activity was engaged to improve the lot of the average investor?

Other factors on the international landscape also further hammered the stock market. Declining economies, unstable governments, faltering businesses and business transactions, wars and skirmishes all impacted the financial world. The "trickle down" effect hammered the nation's investors, too.

My objective in writing this chapter has been to give you some real-world insight, perspective, and most importantly, sound financial planning advice on where and why you should invest your money in certain areas. Even if you agree with my analysis, you may still be drawn to the stock market. That's okay. I'm there, too. However, I strongly encourage you to adopt my conservative approach. Your absolute maximum investment in stocks should be no more than 5 – 15 percent of your total net worth. I believe it's far more prudent to limit your investment to no more than ten percent of your net worth. This is not to say that I'm swearing off the stock market totally or forever. Higher levels of investment might be practical in future years when the market bounces back. But while the economy is still suspect, it's wise to have as little financial exposure as possible. To invest more is to roll some mighty big dice.

Real Estate is the Real Deal

Real estate investments are superior to owning stocks. This is the area in which to invest 75 percent or more of your net worth. The options are remarkably varied, from raw land to residential dwellings to office buildings. Your financial returns are far more likely to remain in the positive column, too. If you live in one of the four states featured in this book and if you acquire a diversified portfolio of real estate holdings, you may have absolutely no interest in stocks or mutual funds. You'll be too busy earning far bigger, better and more exciting returns on those investments to bother with something as risky as the stock market.

In following chapters I will discuss all of my preferred real estate investments and how you can acquire that diversified portfolio in four of the finest states in the Union.

Chapter Three

Why Shouldn't I Invest in the Stock Market Now?

I hear this all the time. People have made so much money over such a long time by investing in stocks and mutual funds that they believe the ride will never end. Well, it's over for now, folks. Whenever someone asks me the question, "Should I invest in the stock market now?" my answer is always the same:

"No!"

"Absolutely, beyond a doubt, no!

"Heck no!"

Before we get into the details of real estate, it's important to really understand why the attraction of stocks and mutual funds can lead investors to financial disaster. Of course, you don't have to take my advice and if after reading this book you still want to invest in stocks and mutual funds, you can't say you were not warned.

However, if you're still of a mind to invest hard-earned money in an easy-to-lose gamble, please heed my advice. Take the time to look before you leap. My recommendation is to limit such investments in stocks to between five and 15 percent of your net assets. To invest more is to trust too much to luck and the uncertainties of an unsettled (and often unsettling) stock market.

Stay completely away from mutual funds. Avoid them like the plague. The mutual fund industry has taken a number of major hits since 2000 arrived and it's still punchy from the blows. Like a boxer hammered with one too many uppercuts to his jaw, the market is still swinging, but not connecting with very many solid hits. In a surprisingly short period of time many mutual funds have merged or simply closed. And as I'm writing this, word of major financial scandals hits the news almost every week.

The nation's mutual fund industry is valued at just under $7 *trillion*. With that much money in play, you'd expect some problems here and there. But many people were stunned by the scope of an illegal trading scandal that could cost small investors billions of dollars annually. Just how bad this mess is isn't known as this book is being written. Criminal charges as well as civil charges are being considered for some of the country's top corporate officials.

New York State's Attorney General charges that Bank of America allowed a hedge fund to make illegal trades. Janus funds, Strong funds, and Banc One funds were cited for permitting trades that "siphoned" profits from small investors and funneled them to some of the "big guys. Although not admitting to guilt, one of the companies, Canary Capital Partners, agreed to $30 million in restitution and a $10 million fine. Bank of America canned a number of employees and one of their security brokers was charged with larceny and security fraud. I don't believe that a company agrees to pay huge fines or fires top personnel because things were going right.

Scandal is now commonplace when it comes to news coverage of the stock market. Here's a recent headline from the business section of my newspaper, "First big trials in Wall Street scandals to start." The AP story covers former Tyco chief Dennis Kozlowski and former financial chief Mark Swartz. Kozlowski, and others, are charged with looting their company of $600 million and that he and Swartz also arranged for $84 million in unauthorized bonuses. That's in addition to their already high salaries and bonus packages.

The headline that greeted me in this morning's newspaper (11/18/03) was "Morgan Stanley agrees to fine - $50 mil to settle mutual-fund charges." According to the SEC, Morgan Stanley steered clients to "preferred" mutual funds, which just happened to be paying millions of dollars in commissions – a "firm-wide failure" in disclosure practices.

What's the point? Well, if you're considering investing in mutual funds you should consider the business ethics of the people and the companies with whom you'll be placing your money. It's not inappropriate to ask if these guys have any ethics at all.

At a minimum, two very important groups of professionals are in place to protect the "small fry" investors, the folks who were burned so badly in this scandal. They are, first, the corporate officers and the directors of the mutual fund companies. Part of their job is to take care of *all* investors, not just the folks with deep pockets. I should add that it's part of their job to know what's going on in the fund, to be honest, to conduct business with integrity, to…perhaps I should send them a copy of the Boy Scout Oath.

Another group charged with protecting investors is the Securities and Exchange Commission. Where were they when all of this was going on? Why was the wrongdoing uncovered by a state district attorney rather than the vaunted SEC? What's worse is that I suspect there's a lot more scandal to be uncovered. That means more investors could be burned.

It's beyond me how anyone can invest in a fund when the two groups of people most responsible for protecting investors have so badly fallen down on the job. These repeated scandals will surely have a negative impact on consumer confidence and may even bring it to new lows. None of this is good for the market or its investors. Even no-load mutual funds (funds sold without a sales commission) aren't attracting new buyers anymore. Clearly, at least some investors are seeing the tarnish appearing on the gold.

As I've already indicated, there will come a time when my "don't buy now" advice is no longer necessary, but that time is most certainly not now and I doubt very seriously if it will arrive in the near future.

Sometimes investors make investing decisions harder than necessary. Often they'll even define their choices in terms that dramatically limit their options. Every now and then it's a good idea to return to the basics, to go back to ground zero and start all over – or at least begin thinking with a fresh, free and clear mind. Making important financial decisions isn't an easy task, even for professionals in the business and people who have been succeeding at it for years or even decades. I have a lot of knowledge about investing and more than forty years of real-world experience, most of it quite successful, too. I still am extremely careful about my investments and never assume that I know it all.

Too many people during the past decade or so invested their money in the stock market with far too little thought about their actions or the consequences of those actions. It's as if they believed that stocks and mutual funds were the financial Holy Grail. Millions of Americans lost 25 – 75 percent of their net worth. The losses were so terrible that many of those millions looking forward to a secure retirement faced dramatic lifestyle changes.

This state is beyond sad. It's tragic. People fell victim to (1) the foolish stock market hype of the late eighties and nineties and (2) to their own willingness to overlook the obvious. They threw caution to the wind and jumped on the band wagon, expecting the happy ride to go on forever. The government didn't help either. I can remember spokesmen from Washington actually bragging that the administration had "ended the business cycle." There would be no more recessions or major downturns in the economy. What nonsense! The market was, is and will always be a rollercoaster. It's a shame that all those investors never paused to consider that every high is followed by a fall, often a rapid and painful one.

Worse than that, the real risk takers borrowed money on "margin" in an effort to hit an even bigger jackpot. What many of them got was bankruptcy, shattered dreams, and a radically altered view of their "golden years."

My view isn't one based on hindsight. My book *Be Money Smart in Real Estate, Investments and Insurance* was published in 2001. I warned then against putting too much investment capital in stocks and mutual funds. I've been at the investment "game" for more than 40 years and I've never understood how people who are very intelligent in most areas could be so foolish in financial matters by placing so much faith and money in the stock market. Anyone who has ever done any reading at all in economic history should know better.

For example, I'd be offering a rock solid investment in real estate, a first mortgage that was completely safe and secure and one that would pay an eight percent annual return. People practically laughed in my face. "Why, Bob, I can get 20 percent, 30 percent or better playing the stock market!"

And that was true – for a while. Of course, we all know that "all good things must come to an end" and this bandwagon was stopped in its tracks by an awful smashup. Please, learn from their mistakes. I must be very, very candid here. *The vast majority of investors who hold stocks and/or mutual funds should get out completely or at least reduce the size of that investment to a small percentage of their net assets.* That's the policy I espouse and the one I practice. At the moment, you couldn't even pay me to buy a mutual fund.

I do actually enjoy owning individual stocks. After a lifetime of studying the market, subscribing to top investment publications such as *Valueline* and *Standard & Poor's Services*, and having taken several courses in the school of hard knocks, I feel confident in doing so. Still, I stay close to a self-imposed limit of five percent of my total net assets. It just boggles my mind to think that intelligent investors would pursue any other course when it makes so much sense (common, financial, etc.) to place the majority of their investments in a safe and secure diversified portfolio of real estate. At least 75 percent of your investments should be put to work in this way.

Despite what your financial advisors might say, despite the over-confidence that is often pumped out of Washington, D.C., and despite any rose colored glasses you might be wearing, take a few moments to honestly answer a few questions. Be open and frank with yourself and I believe you'll gain some genuine insight that will prove most beneficial to your financial future.

1. What logical reason do I have for investing in stocks and/or mutual funds?

2. Do I invest because a stockbroker or financial advisor recommends investing?

3. Do I subscribe to any professional services, such as *Valueline* or *Standard & Poor's*, that provide factual and unbiased information on stocks and companies?

4. Do I sell stocks when they are declining in value?

5. Do I ever sell or do I just buy and hold?

6. Have I bought load mutual funds?

7. How much of my total net worth is invested in stocks and/or mutual funds?

8. How well have my investments done over the years?

9. How much money did I have in stocks and/or mutual funds as of December 31, 1999?

10. How much money did I have in stocks and/or mutual funds as of December 31, 2002?

11. Did the devastation of the years 2000 – 2002 hurt me financially?

12. Do I still believe that I should own stocks and/or mutual funds?

13. Have I invested much of my total net worth in real estate investments?

14. Can I really trust the nation's CEOs and boards of directors with my money?

15. Can I trust the accounting firms working for large companies considering the amount of fraud and scandal in recent years?

16. Do I believe that a diversified portfolio of various real estate investments is better and safer than stocks and/or mutual funds?

17. Can I trust the securities firms to give fair and impartial recommendations?

18. Am I making my own decisions based on fair and impartial consideration or am I basing important decisions on my emotions?

19. Do I personally research and evaluate investment recommendations given to me by my advisors?

20. How much of my assets are invested in safe and secure real estate ventures?

The problem in a nutshell is that there are so many market variables you have no real control over the status or outcome of your investments. Events that impact companies, countries, or investments that you may not even be involved with could have significant ramifications for your financial future. If Poland or Poulan/Weedeater or polling on consumer confidence take a major hit, your investments could be hurt too.

There are many wonderful companies in America and some have proven to be well worth the investment. That being said, you can no longer afford to "buy and hold." For example, McDonalds was a terrific stock to own and they made a lot of people a lot of money for a lot of years. Investors who got out in time did very well indeed. Those who have held on for the past decade have seen their stock hit a ten-year low. Just think about holding a stock for ten years and then ending up with earnings of zip. (Yes, the company pays a modest dividend, but if you were invested, your principal earned nothing during the past decade.) It's hard for many to believe that such a powerful business institution could experience such a blow, but it did happen. Such dramatic drops continue to happen.

Stock and mutual fund investing can be profitable provided you know the market, study the market, closely follow the market, act appropriately and swiftly when necessary, and that you limit your exposure to five to 15 percent of your total net assets. For most investors that's a big and time consuming task. The results for those who do not put in the time and effort could be devastating. I don't use that term lightly. If you are counting on such investments to provide for a safe and secure financial future, take some time to review the horrific market losses of 2000 through 2002. Many people have seen their dreams wiped out or severely damaged because their losses were so big during those years.

Ask yourself, "Is my financial future worth risking in the stock market?"

"Am I willing to trust my financial security to a market that has wiped out thousands and thousands of fortunes, hopes and dreams within just a few years?"

"Just how big a pair of dice am I really willing to toss?"

Why don't I just take a breather and investigate a more secure future in real estate?

That last one is real important. Real estate offers so many varied opportunities to earn terrific returns, that I think you'd be crazy to give it a pass. For example, you could invest in first mortgages or trust deeds. State Tax Certificates are another wonderful option. These instruments vary state-by-state, but basically the investor earns interest on property in which the owner isn't current on his or her property taxes. It's one of the most lucrative real estate investments you can possibly make. Double-digit returns are possible in most states.

If you look at the situation logically, there's just no reason to put more than five to 15 percent of your net assets into the stock market. To do otherwise is to take what I view as an unfounded risk, a financially dangerous one. Limit your exposure to the stock market so you can enjoy the unlimited opportunities offered by real estate: first and second mortgages, first and second trust deeds, state tax certificates, apartments, hotels, raw land, office buildings, industrial buildings, mini-warehouses, mobile home parks, shopping centers, real estate investment trusts, and... and...and...

The list continues. And so do the profits. Real estate investments are the only way to invest your money in safe, secure and high-yielding income-producing financial vehicles. There are so many options, that you can pick and choose an area(s) that is a perfect fit for your bank account, level of expertise and experience, and interests. That's goes double for Arizona, Florida, Nevada and Texas. If you live there, invest there, or just visit there genuine opportunity is truly "right under your feet."

Chapter Four

The Case Against Owning Mutual Funds

How can anyone ever trust their fund managers, the boards of directors, or virtually anyone else in a responsible position with a mutual fund? In early September, 2003 New York State Attorney General Eliot Spitzer rocked the financial world with allegations of trading abuses in the mutual fund industry. And the rock keeps on rolling. As I write this book it seems that there's a new scandal, a new allegation, or a new fine and corporate apology hitting the newspapers every week. Spitzer called it a "cesspool" and he's right. These scandals are embarrassing for some companies, costly for most of them, and possibly the end of the line for many others. Here's a sampling of what's been going on.

- Spitzer kicked things into high gear when in September, 2003 he settled with hedge fund Canary Capital for mutual fund trading abuses. Four fund companies were implicated: Janus Capital, Strong Financial, Bank of America, and Bank One.

- Scandal-tarred Putnam Investments, which has $272 billion in assets, named a new management team in an attempt to restore investor confidence. Lawrence Lasser, Putnam's CEO since 1987 recently resigned under pressure.

- On November 4, 2003 regulators accused seven former Prudential Securities employees of using dozens of fake identities to evade mutual fund rules against market timing, and thereby reaping enormous illegal profits.

- Five former Boston based Prudential brokers and two managers were named in a civil securities travel fraud case by Massachusetts regulators and the Securities and Exchange Commission. Three brokers made nearly $5 million in commissions in 2002 alone, according to the SEC.

- In October, 2003 the SEC surveyed the 88 largest mutual fund firms for market timing allegations. Half of the fund companies had such agreements with favored clients.

These and other revelations (current and future) are merely the tip of the financial iceberg. New charges are surely already in the works. Just look at this blockbuster. The National Association of Securities Dealers and the SEC have cracked down on widespread abuses in mutual fund sales practices. The NASD states that the average overcharge was $243 and that some investors were gouged for as much as $10,000. The NASD estimates that at least $86 million is owed to investors for 2001 and 2002. Look for all kinds of allegations of wrongdoing by many mutual fund companies over the next several years.

Other problems with owning mutual funds are (1) the high sales charges by load funds and (2) on-going management fees. Add in the fact that *most mutual funds have lost money for their investors during the past three years* and you can see why it is hard for me to find a good reason to invest money in them. If, after reading all that, you still want to invest in the market, at least limit your exposure to no more than 10 – 15 percent of your total net worth in stocks only. All you need to do is to buy 15 or 20 good stocks from a discount broker. That way you essentially build your own mutual fund – one that you control.

You may be one of those fortunate investors whose mutual funds have performed well at various times. That's great, but think about this: time has caught up with the mutual fund market. You will be better served by eliminating them from your portfolio. If you're one of the 80 million Americans who lost 50 to 80 percent of your hard-earned money in the market decline that began in Spring of 2000 you really don't want to repeat that experience, do you?

Investors were spoiled and became greedy in the anything-goes 1990s. Of course, that attitude blew up in their faces when the reality of the new century landed on their doorstep. That run up moved faster than even the super heated bull market of the Roaring Twenties. If you will remember your history, that roar was replaced with howls of pain when The Great Depression brought the world to a crash.

The last thing you want is your money invested in an industry that is under siege. Today regulators are turning over every possible rock in the mutual fund industry and they don't like what they're finding. Please heed my advice. Be extremely careful and limit your exposure in the stock market. Avoid mutual funds altogether. Whatever slithers from under those rocks just might give you a painful and perhaps a financially fatal bite.

Chapter Five

An Overview of Real Estate in the Big Four States

I believe you can find good real estate deals just about any place, but clearly some places offer more opportunities than others. And some places offer *great* opportunities in real estate. Arizona, Florida, Nevada and Texas lead the list hands down as far as I'm concerned. Certainly you can conduct real estate transactions in those states from any location, even other states of the Union, but if you live in one of them you have an automatic leg up on the competition. Being on the scene means you can get information faster, verify that information in person if necessary, and enact your response perhaps before the competition can ever really get moving. Take advantage of your advantage.

You still have to be aggressive, a real go-getter. You have to keep abreast of what's going on in your community, region and the entire state or perhaps in all four states if your plans are that expansive. A successful real estate investor stays on top of the situation so that he or she always comes out on top of that situation. Read the national financial newspapers and magazines to see how national and international events will impact local economies. We're in an era of global markets and something that happens on the Pacific Rim, in Europe, Africa or in any number of economies could have a direct impact on real estate in your local market and your personal fortune.

Pay attention to your local and regional publications, too, especially the financial sections. Keep an eye on the real estate classified ads to see if you can spot any emerging trends. Each of the four states has its own business magazine. You should subscribe to the one(s) that apply to your plans. In the case of the neighboring states of Arizona and Nevada, you'll probably want to subscribe to both. Pay particular attention to any real estate sources available to you, including fellow investors, realtors, brokers, bankers, lawyers, accountants and business people. Which part of a city or region is growing the fastest? Can that growth be sustained? Which areas are new and which ones are in decline? Where are the people and the businesses being drawn? Which locations offer the best opportunities for you to make money in real estate? What's the potential lag time between buying and selling your property? Can you afford the carrying charges on that property over time and still earn a good profit? If you study carefully, evaluate all the angles, and invest with a sound plan, I believe your chances of earning outstanding returns are excellent.

Growing Numbers Grow Profit

Take a few minutes to examine the following table showing the population growth of

Arizona, Florida, Nevada and Texas. I think you'll immediately grasp the potential opportunities for owning profitable real estate in these states.

	1970	1980	1990	2000	1990/2000 Increase
AZ	1,775,399	2,716,546	3,665,228	5,130,630	40%
FL	6,791,418	9,746,961	12,937,926	15,982,378	23.5%
NV	488,738	800,508	1,201,833	1,988,257	66.3%
TX	11,986,655	14,225,513	16,986,510	20,851,620	22.8%

There are eight so-called "super states." These are California, Texas, New York, Florida, Illinois, Pennsylvania, Ohio, and Michigan. They are the "key" states reporters like to focus on during presidential elections for that very reason. Take a look at this change in population chart for those states.

	2000 Population	Percent Change 1990 – 2000
California	33,871,648	13.8%
Texas	20,851,820	22.8%
New York	18,976,457	5.5%
Florida	15,982,378	23.5%
Illinois	12,419,293	8.6%
Pennsylvania	12,281,054	3.4%
Ohio	11,353,140	4.7%
Michigan	9,938,444	6.9%

What do you notice? Of all the super states only Texas, ranked at number two, and Florida, ranked number 4, experienced more than 20% growth from 1990 – 2000. Only California broke into double digits and their numbers were close to half the growth of Florida and Texas. Opportunity thrives where there is growth and in terms of growth, Florida and Texas are in a league of their own compared to the other top six. When experts analyze growth patterns, they note three key factors: location, jobs and climate. Of these eight states, clearly Florida and Texas lead the pack. All the real action is either south or west.

Why isn't California included as one of the "hot" states? That's an excellent question deserving of a straightforward answer. It's a simple matter of supply and demand. Despite the high demand for quality real estate in California, the supply is dwindling and therefore, becoming overpriced. Orange Country, Los Angeles, San Francisco, and San Diego are booming markets, but these areas have little available land for further development. That's not to say you can't make successful real estate deals in California. You can, but there are so many better deals elsewhere, I say "why bother?"

I am totally convinced that the best of the best real estate opportunities in the eight super states will be found in Florida and Texas. That's the way it is now and I don't see that changing in the near future.

Here's something else to consider. A major factor in successful real estate development is the weather. What do the five slow-growth states of New York, Illinois, Pennsylvania, Ohio, and Michigan have in common? Cold winter weather, that's what. What do Arizona, Florida, Nevada and Texas have in common? You guessed it, mild winters. You don't have to be a rocket scientist to see the correlation. Today's America is a highly-mobile society. If someone doesn't particularly like where he (or she) lives, he can pretty much pack up and go.

Times aren't like they were just a hundred years ago when people often never traveled more than a few miles from home throughout their lives. Travel today is easy and relatively inexpensive. Job opportunities are plentiful. Communication with friends and loved ones back home is as close as the nearest post office, telephone or Internet connection. Why shouldn't someone seek better opportunities elsewhere? That's why so many people are moving into these four states.

Now let's look at a few states in the middle of the pack, states with populations in the four to five million range. These states start with Missouri which is ranked number 17 in terms of population.

	2000 Population	1990 – 2000 Increase
17 Missouri	5,595,211	9.3%
18 Wisconsin	5,363,675	9.6%
19 Maryland	5,296,486	10.8%
20 Arizona	5,130,632	40.0%
21 Minnesota	4,919,479	12.4

22 Louisiana	4,468,976	5.9%
23 Alabama	4,447,100	10.1%
24 Colorado	4,301,261	30.6
25 Kentucky	4,041,769	9.7%

I don't ever mean to imply that you can't find real estate opportunities in states other than Arizona, Florida, Nevada and Texas. That's not the case. Good deals can be made just about anywhere. My point is simply that you can find a *lot* of *great* real estate opportunities in these four states. Look at the above chart. At a 40 percent growth in the past decade, Arizona has a commanding lead on every state. The only state coming remotely close is the great and beautiful State of Colorado, but real estate investors run into problems there, also.

Just as California is behind the booming super states of Florida and Texas, Colorado shares the same distinction compared to Arizona in the middle level states. Again, I know that Colorado offers numerous "under your feet" opportunities for those who live or invest there. I realize that you can find investments in every part of the state. Still, I recommend Arizona. The numbers favor the more western state. For one thing, and it's a big factor, Colorado has some of the most unpredictable weather anywhere and winters can be a long and uncomfortable stretch. Real estate development can grind to a halt in some parts of the state for months at a time. If the bundled up winter skiers in Arizona's high country had a powerful enough telescope they could look down on massive construction for homes, businesses and industry throughout the state throughout the winter. The current construction boom continues all year round.

You can't really make things happen when nothing's happening. Something's always happening in Arizona.

Let's take a look at some of the states with smaller populations. We'll start with number 34, Utah.

	2000 Population	1990 – 2000 Increase
34 Utah	2,233,169	29.6%
35 Nevada	1,998,257	66.3%
36 New Mexico	1,619,046	20.1
37 West Virginia	1,808,344	0.8%
38 Nebraska	1,711,263	8.4%
39 Idaho	1,293,953	28.5%
40 Maine	1,274,923	3.8%
41 New Hampshire	1,235,786	11.4%

Again, one of the states I recommend leads the rest of the pack and by a large margin. Idaho is number two on the list, Nevada has experienced more than twice that amount of growth and more than three times the growth of the next nearest state, Utah. People don't move someplace in such massive quantities because it's a bad deal. Like metal filings to a magnet, people are attracted to good locations, good jobs, and a good climate.

Just like California and the other big states and Colorado in the middle range, Utah is a runner-up in the list of smaller states. Utah has certainly experienced its share of growth and for sheer beauty, it's one of the nation's most spectacular. Still, with a growth of only 29.6%, Utah can't hold a candle to Nevada. Reno, Lake Tahoe, and, of course, Las Vegas are top tourist destinations for people from all over the world. Individuals, couples and families just love the excitement found in these cities. Las Vegas is especially popular for its casinos, live entertainment, big name performing talent, and exquisite restaurants.

Regardless of your current interest level in Arizona, Florida, Nevada or Texas, I urge you to invest some time and look carefully at them as potential avenues for real estate investment. Certainly there are many opportunities "right under your feet" wherever your feet are planted. Yet your chances of finding quantity and quality investments in these four blockbuster states are much, much greater than in any of the other states of the Union. As the saying goes, it's wise to fish where the fish are biting. Take a business trip or even a vacation to get a personal look. If you have friends or relatives, call them up and book a week or at least a long weekend with them. Do what you have to do to get a first-hand look at the tremendous opportunities awaiting you.

Smart real estate investment in these four states is about as close to a "can't miss" proposition as I've ever seen. Arizona, Florida, Nevada, and Texas have lots of room to expand for residential, commercial and industrial development. They have excellent locations now and for the foreseeable future. Each one is a leading provider of jobs. Employers of all types need all types of people to fill those positions. Blue-collar workers, white-collar workers, high-tech engineers and scientists, craftsmen, tradesmen, day workers, entrepreneurs, and corporate leaders are all in demand and there's no end to that demand in sight. The climate is excellent and varied in all four states, affording residents and guests a wide variety of business and recreational options. All of these factors and more add up to one thing – fantastic opportunities for real estate investors. Why don't you reach out and grasp your share?

Chapter Six

Arizona
"The Grand Canyon State"

Fact File:

Location: Southwestern United States bordered by Utah on the north, Mexico to the south, New Mexico to the east, and Nevada and California to the west.

Size: 114,006 square miles.

Population: According to the 2000 census there are more than 5,000,000 people living in Arizona.

Capital City: Phoenix in the south central area of the state.

Interstates: I-40, I-10 and I-8 run east/west and I-17 and I-19 run north/south.

Largest Cities: Phoenix, Tucson, Mesa, Glendale, Scottsdale, Chandler, Tempe, Gilbert, Peoria, Flagstaff, and Yuma. Except for Tucson, Flagstaff and Yuma, the others form part of a metropolitan area known as the Valley of the Sun.

State Bird: Cactus Wren

State Flower: Saguaro cactus bloom, a white and yellow flower appearing on the tall and stately cactus unique to Arizona.

State Tree: Palo Verde, a tree with green bark and bright yellow flowers.

State Song: "Arizona"

Admitted to the Union: February 14, 1912 as the 48th state.

The Grand Canyon State, with New Mexico, Colorado and Utah, is one of the "Four Corners" states. All four touch at far northeastern Arizona, the only such place in the United States. Arizona is divided into three distinct areas. The land here can only be described as dramatic, powerful and exciting. That goes for the real estate deals, too.

The Colorado Plateau makes up most of the northern part of the state. Here you'll find some of the state's most spectacular scenery, including the Grand Canyon, Canyon de Chelly (pronounced dee shay), and Monument Valley's striking landscapes made famous in many of John Ford's western films. Humphreys Peak, near Flagstaff, is the state's highest mountain at more than 12,000 feet above sea level. Other striking features include the Painted Desert, the Petrified Forest, and the Mogollon (pronounced muggy-on) Rim, a 2,000 foot ridge that runs across about two-thirds of the state and into New Mexico's Mogollon Mountains.

Central Arizona is a mountainous area covered by dense forests and is considered a summer vacation or weekend "escape pod" for the desert dwellers to the south. The Verde River runs north/south and the southern Salt River runs east/west. The strikingly beautiful "Red Rock Country" around Sedona is one of the state's largest tourism draws.

The Basin and Range to the south is Sonoran Desert country, perhaps most noted for the tall, green saguaro cactus with its upturned arms. The east/west Gila River runs across the state and eventually flows into the Colorado River. The lowest spot in Arizona, 70 feet above sea level, is along the Colorado. Thanks to irrigation, first practiced hundreds of years before the arrival of westerners, much of the desert area has been turned into productive farmland.

Arizona has a dry climate with the desert areas averaging only six to eight inches of rain a year. Even the mountainous areas receive only an average about 30 inches of rain a year. Due to the wide differences in elevation, temperatures can vary to a remarkable degree.

People in the Valley of the Sun (Phoenix-Mesa metro area) have been known to dash up to Flagstaff for a morning of snow skiing and then to dash back to The Valley to enjoy a brisk afternoon dip in their swimming pool. Summers in the desert often reach and hold at 100 degrees Fahrenheit for days or even weeks at a time. Nighttime temperatures in the mountains can dip to 32 degrees Fahrenheit. I-40 in the northern portion of the state has been shut down due to snow at the same time people in Phoenix or Tucson are playing golf in shorts and polo shirts.

Key Attractions

"Points of interest" is a phrase found in many guidebooks and it refers to any number of attractions found in the area covered. These areas are of particular interest to real estate savvy people because of Cooley's "People-Pressure Principle." Attractions *attract.* People moving into a place need a place to move in to and that creates a real estate market. For example, Tombstone is a very small town built around a single industry, tourism. There is a lot of raw land available at reasonable prices all around that part of the country. Because people are fascinated with the town's colorful history, especially the famous gunfight at the OK corral, people from all over the world make the pilgrimage. Tombstone gets a lot more "foot traffic" than the average small town and that fact could create a real estate bonanza for some smart buyer. Arizona is filled with such opportunities.

Phoenix. There's no greater example of American entrepreneurship than Phoenix. A few decades ago Phoenix was just another average size American city. Today it's the fifth largest metro area in the nation. The attractions of climate, jobs and location have been working overtime and there's absolutely no indication of a slowdown on the horizon. The city is a remarkable mixture of cultures: Spanish, Mexican, Native American, cowboys, entrepreneurs and "just folks" from all around the globe.

Phoenix is the capital of the state, providing its citizens with more than politics and business. There's an active arts and cultural community which features world-class museums, theaters, a state-of-the-art convention center, professional sports (including a world championship baseball team), an astounding number of top-rated golf courses, outdoor recreation and sporting events, colleges and universities. Despite its "cowboy" image, and there's plenty of that to go around, the city is a sophisticated and cosmopolitan island in the desert.

Agriculture, service industries, high technology, electronics, aerospace, research and development, and a broad industrial base make for a stable economy. Area crops include cotton, citrus, fruits, olives, and other sub-tropical fruits and vegetables. The state's natural beauty and the metro area's many attractions have created an enormous tourism industry.

Tucson is located in the southern part of Arizona, "the Old Pueblo" as it is called traces its history back to the 1700s. Today it is another of the state's tourism centers, but also a center of culture, the performing arts, sports, and recreational activities. The city's Native American and Spanish roots are evident in its architecture, arts and crafts, cuisine and numerous festivals.

Tucson's industrial base includes its colleges and universities, Davis-Monthan Air Force Base, computer technology, high-tech industries, and agriculture are important industries. The city's population is approximately 500,000.

Sedona is hidden in the stunningly beautiful Red Rock Country north of Phoenix. The combination of the lush growth of Oak Creek Canyon and the prominent fiery red buttes and canyons have attracted settlers and tourists for thousands of years. If you're a fan of western films, you've seen Sedona. *Angel and the Badman, Firecreek, The Rounders,* and *The Quick and the Dead* are just a few examples.

Tourism is very big in Sedona. The natural beauty is ideal for camping, hiking, touring, jeep tours, and even aerial tours by plane, helicopter and hot air balloon. The city is also home to an extraordinary variety of fine artists and galleries. The city is famous for its seven "vortexes," areas through which natural power fields are said to flow.

Flagstaff, located on I-40 and historic Route 66 in the northern part of the state, offers a widely diversified lifestyle. It is the home to Northern Arizona University and has a population of about 53,000. The "City of the Pines" is well named because it is near some truly spectacular mountain vistas, snow skiing areas, and numerous areas for fishing, hunting, hiking and camping. Nearby attractions include the Grand Canyon, Sunset Crater National Monument, and the Coconino National Forest. Many people who live in the desert areas also own summer homes in or near Flagstaff. The air may be crisp and cool, but the real estate deals are frequently hot, hot, hot.

Other fascinating attractions of Arizona cities include: the upscale environment of Scottsdale, "the West's most Western town;" the resort community of Prescott; Tombstone, the "town too tough to die;" the old mining community of Bisbee; and the ghosts and artisans of Jerome.

Arizona's People

Western states have a track record for phenomenal growth and at number two on the list Arizona is one of the leaders. The population increased 40 percent between the 1990 and 2000 census and as of this writing there doesn't appear to be any slow down in that pattern. The state's diversified economy attracts many people looking for good jobs at good wages. Others are attracted to the dry climate and spectacular scenery. The climate also attracts seniors and retirees and there are a number of well-known retirement communities including Sun City and Sun City West near Phoenix. Basically, there's something for everybody, which make this state an ideal vehicle for real estate investment.

The development of a reliable water supply coupled with the invention of air conditioning brought a boom in population in the latter half of the 20th century. Approximately two thirds of that population is Anglo-American, a large percentage of them newcomers. About a quarter of the population is Hispanic, some of them newcomers and some with family roots dating back to the days when Mexico and even Spain ruled the land. Many of these folks live in the southern part of the state, particularly in border towns such as Douglas, Nogales and Yuma.

Arizona has nearly a quarter of a million Native Americans, the third largest in the nation. The Navajo and their cousins the Apache tribes are the largest, but the state has a varied population including Tohono O'Odham (Papago), Akmiel O'Odham (Pima), Hopi, and Yavapai. Many of these people choose to live on their reservations, such as the Navajo in the north. It is the nation's largest. The Akmiel O'Odham reservation south of Phoenix is the nation's second largest.

African-Americans arrived here generally after the Civil War. They came as soldiers, (many of them among the famous "Buffalo Soldiers"), as farmers and ranchers, and as railroad workers. This group makes up about three percent of the state's population, primarily in Phoenix.

A small group of Asian-Americans, less than 100,000, includes people from China, Japan, Vietnam, Korea and India.

Arizona's History

Men and women wandered throughout Arizona at least 12,000 years ago, but these weren't settlers, rather they followed the tracks of the Wooly Mammoth and other ancient animals. True civilization arrived around 1300 years ago. (The dates vary according to the definition of "culture" and "civilization" and the opinions of experts in archaeology.) Such groups as the Anazazi and Hohokam built homes and villages, established trade networks and produced beautiful works of art. Many of the nation's famous cliff dwellings, ancient adobe "apartment bulidings," are found in Arizona. Until the advent of structural steel, the ancients built the tallest buildings in America. An astounding network of large irrigation canals was built in the Valley of the Sun and many of those are still in use today. Navajo and Apache people arrived around 900 years ago.

Arizona became part of New Spain around A.D. 1540 as the conquistadors searched for gold and the padres searched for souls. Spanish missions began appearing around 1600. Life here was tough, especially considering the fierce defense put up by the Navajo and the Apache. Even the peaceful Pima revolted in the late 18th century. Few of the Spanish people settled permanently. Mexico eventually won its independence and Arizona became part of that nation in 1821. Still, there was little settlement.

A few American trappers and mountain men traveled Arizona, but few Anglos came to know the state until gold was discovered in California. Arizona was on the route toward the gold fields and many men stopped along the way or remembered the potential here and returned. The United States won Arizona in the Mexican War (1846 – 1848) and the territory was expanded by the Gadsden Purchase in 1853. Gold, silver and copper were discovered as were fields for planting and ranchland for grazing and for the first time since the ancient ones, people began to settle down.

The Civil War devastated what would one day become Arizona. A few battles were fought here, but mostly the military marched to the battles in the East. The population declined as a result of a loss of manpower and renewed Native American warfare. Arizona Territory was formed in 1863, which kept the area within the Union, even though much of the population favored the Southern cause.

Indian warfare dominated the headlines for more than two decades after the Civil War. Leaders such as Cochise and Geronimo are still well-known names today and heroes to many people throughout the world. This was the time of Wyatt Earp and Doc Holiday, but also of increased mining, farming, ranching and economic expansion. The end of the Indian wars is generally agreed to have occurred with the surrender of Geronimo in 1886.

The continental United States became a complete entity in 1912 when Arizona became the 48th state. The state's population remained small, but it continued to grow. Many of the wild rivers were tamed, bringing power, irrigation and recreation to residents and tourists.

Following World War II the desert began to "heat up" in terms of population growth, job opportunities, and real estate deals. The economy began a transition to manufacturing, which included many high-tech industries. The dams made water available and air conditioning made the climate easy to handle and the state began an economic boom that continues today.

Arizona's Business Climate

Arizona's business has evolved from ancient farming to modern farming and ranching, mining, and manufacturing. Those are still important elements of the economy, but they are waning in comparison to the service sector. Approximately 80 percent of the state's workforce is employed by a service industry. This economy is diversified and includes, retail shops and stores, banks and savings and loans,

53

insurance companies, corporate headquarters of numerous businesses and industries, maintenance and repair facilities for everything from a toaster to a passenger jet or satellite, and just about any kind of service business you could come up with.

Real estate has been, is, and is expected to be very strong for some time. Buying and selling opportunities run the full gamut. Raw land is available in the desert, high desert, plateau, mountains, rolling hills, gentle valleys, and you can even purchase old mining claims. Homes, condos, town homes, shopping centers, warehouses, industrial sites and parks, high-rise buildings, and...well, you name it and it's here.

A lot of service industries are tailored to military installations such as Luke Air Force Base near Phoenix, Ft. Huachuca near Sierra Vista in the south, and the Yuma Proving Grounds. Arizona State University, the University of Arizona, and Northern Arizona University are also large employers.

Naturally, tourism is a major industry bringing in approximately $10 billion annually. The state boasts some of the most famous national parks in the nation, internationally known resorts, extensive opportunities for golf and other recreational outlets. "City life" can be as varied as an evening of fine dining and entertainment in the nation's fifth largest city (Phoenix) to a quiet bed and breakfast weekend at a revived ghost town such as Jerome or an afternoon stroll through an authentic ghost town.

Manufacturing is found state-wide, but is centered and concentrated in Phoenix and Tucson. Major industries provide major aircraft components, aircraft parts, missile technology, space vehicles, automobile safety devices, computers, computer chips, and computer components.

Agriculture has been part of the state's economy for nearly 2,000 years. Once water became readily available through extensive irrigation, all types of products have been grown here. Cotton is the principle crop and because of the long growing season under the desert sun Pima cotton is recognized as one of the finest in the world. Other crops include lettuce, figs, oranges, grapefruit and other citrus crops, watermelons, grapes, olives, potatoes, tomatoes, and cauliflower.

Ranching is still a profitable business, although many of the older and larger ranches are being broken up for land development. Cattle, sheep and angora goats make up the principle herds. Most cattle ranching takes place in the central portion of the state and the Navajo still herd sheep on their reservation in the north.

Mining is no longer the industrial giant it was a few decades ago, but it is still a vital and important industry. Arizona is sometimes called the "Copper State" and it produces more of that metal than any other state in the Union. Some gold and silver mining continues, but mainly as a byproduct of copper mining. Prospecting by individuals, families and clubs is a very popular hobby in mineral rich parts of the state. Coal, crushed stone, gravel and sand are also important mining industries.

Chapter Seven

Florida
"The Sunshine State"

Fact File:

Location: Southeastern United States, bordered by the Atlantic coast on the east and the Gulf of Mexico to the west, and Alabama and Georgia to the north.

Size: 53,927 square miles.

Population: 15,982,378

Capital City: Tallahassee

Interstates: I-10, I-4, and I-75 run east/west and I-75 and I-95 run north/south.

Largest Cities: Tallahassee, Jacksonville, Orlando, St. Petersburg, Miami, Tampa,

Hollywood, Clearwater, and Fort Lauderdale.

State Bird: Mockingbird.

State Flower: Orange blossom.

State Tree: Sable palm.

State Animal: Florida Panther.

State Song: "Old Folks at Home."

Admitted to the Union: March 3, 1845 as the 27th state.

Florida's Environment

Florida's beaches are one of the state's primary tourist attractions and Floridians can accommodate a lot of tourists. The state has more coastline (1,350 miles) than any other state save the much larger Alaska. Florida is "close" to the oceans and seas in more ways than one. With its highest point at only 345 feet, most of the state is just a few feet above sea level.

Three distinct land forms add variety to the environmental mix. Northern Florida is hilly and deeply forested with pine trees. This area has much in common with the contiguous states of Georgia and Alabama and much of the Deep South. This narrow stretch of land running east/west is known as the Florida Panhandle because on maps it actually appears to be a handle jutting westward off the main body of the state.

Central Florida features rivers, lakes and a soil ideal for growing citrus. The groves of oranges, lemons, and grapefruit are common sites. The state is so well-known for its citrus product, that it adopted the orange blossom as its state flower. Central Florida generally runs from the northeastern part of the state down to the famous Lake Okeechobee, a 700 square mile shallow body of water at the far southern end of the central area of the state. The south/north St. Johns River also flows through central Florida.

Southern Florida is dominated by wetlands. In the days before political correctness these areas were simply called swamps. There are few people, few towns and few roads within this expanse. Most of southern Florida's population is found along the coastlines facing the Atlantic to the east, the Straits of Florida to the south, and the Gulf of Mexico to the West. Continental America's southern most city, Key West, is located at the tip of a chain of islands to the south known as the Florida Keys. These islands are connected to each other and the mainland by the 106 mile long Overseas Highway.

Florida's climate is marked by humidity and warm temperatures year round. Spring and summer bring heavy rainfalls to swell the creeks, bayous, rivers and lakes. Temperatures in the interior are warmer than on the coasts where sea breezes cool things down a bit. If you've ever followed your local weather or are a fan of the Weather Channel, you know that the state is hit, sometimes hammered, with hurricanes each year. Hurricanes produce heavy rains, powerful winds, and huge waves that can cause terrible damage as they move in and equally terrible damage as they fall back toward the seas. Mild hurricanes are often endured with boarded up windows and doors, but major events may call for the evacuation of large populations.

Considering that so much of Florida is wetland, hills and forests it's not surprising that a lot of wildlife claim the state as their home. Alligators wander the length of the entire state and as civilization encroaches on their territory contact between "gator" and human is becoming more common. The manatee is a mammal able to swim in salt and fresh water. These larges animals have long, flat tails, a face that looks something like a walrus (minus the tusks), and are known as "sea cows." A full grown manatee can weigh as much as a ton. Florida is on the flyway for many birds. Many others migrate to and from the state and more tropical birds can be found here than in any other state.

Key Attractions

Let's start with the obvious, *Miami-Miami Beach,* an arresting blend of contemporary, Mediterranean and even art deco architectural styles. There's a very Caribbean flavor to the entire community, an identity reflected in the area's music, people, culture, events and even choice of colors. Miami proper is, of course a tourist center, but it also boasts a broader commercial and industrial base than the more tourist-oriented Miami Beach. Most people don't distinguish between the two.

Property values have been rising steadily as the cities expand. A lot of that expansion is due to the hundreds of thousands of Cuban refugees who have transformed much of the area into an even greater economic engine. Other

Spanish-speaking people have followed suit, so much so that the area is often referred to as the new "Ellis Island."

Downtown Miami boasts the highest concentration of international banking interests in the southeastern United States. Miami hosts the world's largest port for cruise ships. The Miami-Dade County air/sea/ground transportation system handles more than five million tons of containerized cargo every year. The airport alone handles more than a million tons of cargo annually.

Orlando is, of course, home to Walt Disney World, SeaWorld, and Universal Studios...and a good bit more. Thanks in large part to the vision of Mickey Mouse's creator, central Florida is now one of the top tourist attractions in the world. It is a place where the proverbial owner of swampland converted his or her muck into bucks, big bucks.

Business activities extend far beyond talking mice and jumping dolphins. Central Florida has for most of the past century been home to many corporate leaders in the space race. Aerospace technology is big here. Real estate, spurred by the tourism boom, is another big business. Computer software, high-technology industries, defense, lasers, telecommunications, electro-optics, and even motion pictures are major players on the economic stage.

Tampa (Tampa, St Petersburg, Clearwater) are perhaps best known for the superior quality of their beautiful, white sand beaches. These alone draw tens of thousands of tourists (and tourist dollars) every year, but there's a lot more to this west coast city. Tampa Bay also goes by the name "Technology Bay" and for good reason. About fifteen percent of the city's population is employed by high-technology industries, such as AT&T, General Electric, Honeywell Avionics, Verizon, Unisys, and others. The Home Shopping Network is even located here.

Almost 200 of America's Fortune 500 companies call the area home. About 23 percent of the state's biomedical manufacturing is conducted here. Other local industries include citrus canning, shrimping, paint manufacturing, brewing (Busch Gardens beat Disney here by more than a decade), phosphate mining, finance, transportation, government, and even the venerable art of cigar making.

Jacsksonville in the far northeast on the Atlantic coast is a busy seaport. It is also a leader in finance, transportation, industry, commerce and culture. Banking, insurance, health and the military also make significant contributions to the economic base. The small town founded in 1562 is now a major city with a population exceeding one million.

Other notable attractions include: *Tallahassee,* which was chosen as the capital in 1823 because of its position midway between St. Augustine and Pensacola; *St. Augustine,* the oldest continually-occupied European settlement in the U.S.; Pensacola, home to the Navy's Blue Angels flying team; the white sand beaches of *Panama City,* and the city of islands, *Fort Lauderdale.*

Florida's People

Of course, the ancient people who pre-dated the Native Americans were here first, chasing the herds of large beasts and living a nomadic lifestyle. The Native Americans were well established by the time the first European explorers arrived. The United States fought three Indian Wars against the Seminoles and if I remember my history correctly they are the only tribe that never signed a peace treaty with the U.S. Government. Although the tribe lost those wars and most of the people were relocated, many fled to Southern Florida where their descendents still live as members of small communities or on reservations.

Other prominent tribes included the forest and swamp-dwelling Calusa who were hunters and fishermen. The Timucua and Tequesta were representatives of the mound building cultures that dominated the Southeastern United States for centuries. Many of their burial mounds are still in existence and are part of state parks celebrating this element of Florida civilization.

Although "discovered" and settled by Spanish explorers in the 1500s, Florida's largest Hispanic group is made up of fairly recent arrivals. Hundreds of thousands of Cubans, 300,000 in 1961 alone, fled the communist government of Fidel Castro which seized control of the island in 1959. Most of them live in South Florida and many of those reside in or near Miami. Miami's Little Havana is famous for its entrepreneurship, Latin music, entertainment, food and the zest for life of its citizens. Cubans comprise approximately 17 percent of the state's population.

About 15 percent of Floridians are African-American, many the descendents of runaway slaves who arrived before the United States was created. The Spanish rulers held a more lenient position on slavery at that time than the inhabitants of the British colonies. Slaves were still a part of the economy and many were brought in from Cuba, the Dominican Republic, and the Antilles. In more recent years, Florida's healthy economy has attracted African Americans from throughout the United States. As those of you who watch the news programs know, Florida is still a destination for refugees seeking escape from economic slavery and harsh governments.

A lot of those refugees come from the impoverished island of Haiti. Bahamians, who began arriving about a hundred years ago, comprise another relatively large segment of the population.

More than three quarters of Florida's population is white. Some are descendents of early settlers, but many more arrived in more recent times seeking the benefits of a sound economy and a warm climate.

Florida's History

Florida's recorded history began with the arrival of Spanish explorers in the 1500s. The first was Juan Ponce de Leon who is famous for his search for the fabled fountain of youth, but who was more likely looking for gold just like everybody else. He arrived in 1513, followed by Hernando de Soto in 1539. St. Augustine, founded in 1565, is the oldest city in the United States. (Note: the Hopi residents of Oraibi in Arizona, who have lived in that town for more than a thousand years, dispute this claim and with good reason.)

The English acquired Florida from Spain in 1763 only to lose it back to Spain after the American Revolutionary War. Florida was given to the new nation of the United States in 1821. Statehood was granted in 1845. Plantation life, and slavery, dominated much of the economy and Florida joined the Confederacy during the Civil War. Florida rejoined the Union in 1868 with a constitution granting voting rights to its African-American citizens.

Growth and then decline marked the next eight or so decades. Early on, visionaries realized the potential for commerce and industry within this tropical state. Many of the swamps were drained. Railroads connecting the state's inhabitants with each other and the rest of the country were built. Miami Beach became a tourist Mecca, initiating a trend that continues today. People began migrating toward this new economic opportunity. Then two disasters began a long period of decline. Hurricanes in the 1920s devastated many communities across the state. Thousands of people were killed and the property damage was enormous. Economic disaster followed natural disaster when the Great Depression hit in 1929.

As with the rest of the nation, Florida's economy did not really bounce back until the advent of World War II. Military training bases were enlarged or established. Florida's key location was of primary concern, so additional military attention was provided. Many of these service people were attracted by the climate and the prospect for good jobs and stayed after the war. Miami, Tampa, Pensacola and other communities began to bloom.

Two other major "booms" occurred in the 1960s. The influx of Cuban refugees brought new people, new ideas, and "new blood" into the state. The success stories of these exiles, many of them arriving with only the clothes on their backs, are an inspiration. The second boom came with the arrival of a man and a mouse. Walt Disney built Disney World near Orlando and today that city is the number one tourist attraction in the world.

Florida's Business Climate

As you might expect, the man and the mouse, Florida's warm climate, its miles and miles of beautiful beaches, its friendly people, and numerous other attractions make the state a top destination for tourists from all over the world. Approximately 50 million tourists arrive every year making tourism the state's largest industry.

Agriculture is still big, especially in central and southern parts of the state where the soil is ideal for growing a wide variety of crops and for raising cattle and thoroughbred horses. Oranges are a major crop. Others include grapefruit, lemons, limes, tangerines, almonds, pecans, peanuts, avocados, bananas, strawberries, melons, tomatoes, soybeans and tobacco. Florida produces more sugar cane than any other state save Hawaii.

Being virtually surrounded by oceans and seas, commercial fishing is a major industry. Important catches include red snapper, shrimp, lobster, oysters, clams and crabs.

As the center for so much raw food production, one of Florida's largest industries is food processing, especially for frozen and canned juices, processed vegetables and fish. The location of America's primary rocket launching facility,

Cape Canaveral, also launched a major aero-space industry. Rockets for peaceful and military purposes are designed, built, tested and launched here.

Florida also produces one-third of the world's supply of phosphate, an ingredient essential to fertilizer production.

Florida, like the other three states featured in this book, has seen raw land blossom. Large tracts of land about which people said, "I wouldn't give you a plug nickel for it" are now selling at hefty prices per square foot.

Chapter Eight

Nevada
"The Silver State"

Fact File:

Location: Southwestern United States bordered by Oregon and Idaho to the north, California to the west and south, and Arizona and Utah to the east.

Size: 109,826 square miles.

Population: 1,998,257.

Capital City: Carson City.

Interstates: I-80 running east/west and I-15 running southwest/northeast.

Largest Cities: Las Vegas and North Las Vegas, Reno, Henderson, Sparks, Carson City, Elko, Boulder City, Mesquite and Fallon.

State Bird: Mountain Bluebird.

State Flower: Sagebrush.

State Tree: Bristlecone Pine.

State Song: "Home Means Nevada"

Admitted to the Union: October 31, 1864 as the 36th state.

Nevada's Environment

Nevada is a dry, rugged land marked by deserts and mountains. The state boasts more than 300 mountain ranges. Among these are Sierra Nevada, Monitor Range, Toiyabe Range, and the Humbolt Range. Except for its northwestern corner, Nevada lies within the Great Basin, a 215,000 square mile area in which all the rivers are contained. None flow to the ocean or into any other river. Still, it's an incredibly dry area and even when water arrives it dries quickly.

The southern tip of the state is within the Mojave Desert which receives less than five inches of rainfall a year. Flora and fauna include Joshua trees, sagebrush, cacti, bighorn sheep, bobcats, and rattlesnakes. Nevada's lowest point at 470 feet above sea level is in this area. The highest point, the 13,000 ft. Boundary Peak is to the northwest on the border with California.

The Columbia Plateau is located in the northeastern portion of the state. It is a high, flat area where little more than grasses and shrubs grow. The Sierra Nevada mountain range, long a barrier to exploration and settlement, is located in the west-central section of the state and is mostly in California. It is forested with pine trees. Its glaciers and massive snowstorms caused worry, misery and often death to early westward explorers and migrants.

You might hear of Nevada's "sinks." These are lowland areas into which rivers flow. For example, the Humbolt River flows into the Humbolt Sink and the Carson River flows into the Carson Sink. The massive construction that is Hoover Dam creates Lake Mead from the blocked flow of the Colorado River along the state's eastern border. Lake Tahoe, the nation's largest mountain lake, is within the Sierra Nevada. Other lakes include Pyramid Lake in the northwest and Walker Lake in the central west.

With the deserts averaging only five inches of rainfall a year and other parts of the state reaching only nine inches per year, Nevada is the clear champion for driest state in the Union. Only the snows found in the Sierra Nevada Mountains provide any real moisture. Temperatures range from the low 30s to more than 90 degrees. Of course, these temperatures can vary considerably according to local conditions.

Las Vegas. Let's face it, many people don't realize there's a state called Nevada around the City of Las Vegas. Considering all the promotion, commercials, motion pictures, and hype it's no wonder the city draws virtually all the attention. Lost Wages. Sin City. Gambleville. The Garden of Neon. All these names revolve around the city's number one attraction – gambling and entertainment. Like Phoenix, Las Vegas has experienced explosive growth in just the latter half of the 20th century and gambling and hospitality-related industries are at the heart of that growth.

Casinos rule in Las Vegas, but numerous lures are used to bring in and hold the gamblers, their friends and families, and even folks who never spend more than "pin money" on the quarter slots. Here you'll find some of the world's most famous live performers putting on some of the world's most expensive and lavish shows. They say there are more headliners and outrageous spectaculars per square mile than in any other city on the face of the Earth.

The numbers tell the story: more than 123,000 hotel rooms for a city with a population of about 500,000 people; more than 35 million tourists came through just in 2001; more than $31.5 billion in tourist dollars; $6 billion in casino revenue; and a "strip" of casinos and casino/hotel/entertainment complexes that continues to amaze the world as it continues to reinvent itself. Las Vegas just keeps on growing and one of the things growing with it is an enormous and active real estate industry.

Reno. Yes, there's another city in Nevada. Reno calls itself "the biggest little city in the world," a reference to the diversity of life, entertainment, and opportunity available to tourist and settler alike. Reno has its share of 24-hour a day casinos, but its economy is a bit more diversified than that of Las Vegas.

Sports and outdoor recreation are big here. Snow skiers enjoy the nearby Sierra Nevada Mountains of California. Boating and even white water rafting are popular during the summer months. The University of Nevada at Reno is a big employer and the city is also a major distribution and merchandising center for the Southwest.

Real estate development is not limited to these two cities. You'll find plenty of opportunity state wide, including: *Carson City*, the state capital; Elko, in the heart of Nevada's cattle country; another gambling center, *Laughlin*, near Arizona; *Boulder City* near Hoover Dam is the only city in the state to prohibit gambling; and *Virginia City* which has done remarkably well in restoring its 1870's gold rush appearance.

The Lake Tahoe area, and the lake itself, are major tourist (and real estate) attractions. Summer activities include hiking, camping, fishing, and water skiing. Winter activities include Snow skiing, snow boarding and other winter sports. Naturally, you'll find gambling in the casinos and all kinds of events, interests and activities in the resort areas and lodges. A huge lake in a desert state is a large draw already, but the other features and benefits of this area make it a real gold mine of a real estate opportunity.

Nevada's People

Although the nomadic Paleo-Indians roamed the land that was to become Nevada, they were a migratory people. Later people began to live in semi-permanent villages and in more recent times true Native Americans emerged. The primary tribes became the Paiute, Bannock, Washoe and Shoshone. Other, smaller groups were scattered across the state. Today the largest tribe is the Washoe and the largest reservation is the Paiute Pyramid Lake Reservation. Nevada has other reservations, although many native people live in or near the cities. About one percent of the population is Native American.

Approximately 65 percent of Nevada's population is white, many of them attracted by the healthy, dry climate, the wide open spaces, job opportunities and the lack of a state income tax. People of European stock began moving to Nevada in large numbers during the 1800s. Different cultures were attracted to different opportunities. The Italians and Irish worked in the silver mines; Germans were attracted to the Carson River where they became farmers; the Basques from France and Spain took up sheep herding; and a group of Mormons arrived from Utah to found the city of Genoa.

Nevada has always attracted Hispanic people. Many of them arrived from Mexico more than a century ago to work the gold and silver mines. Today's Hispanic population blends many nationalities and cultures, including Mexican, Puerto Rican, Cuban, and South American. Approximately 20 percent of the population is Hispanic.

About seven percent of Nevada's population is African-American. The first significant migration of this group didn't occur until the 1930s when an army of workers arrived to construct the Hoover Dam. Sizeable populations of African-Americans are found in Las Vegas, Carson City, Reno and Henderson.

Asian-Americans, about five percent of the population, are Nevada's fastest-growing group and the state is number four of all states in the size of its Asian-American population. The largest sub-group is from the Philippines. There is a substantial Chinese presence, many of them descendents from workers who arrived to help construct the railroads in the 1800s.

Nevada's History

Ancient people crisscrossed the state for at least 10,000 years and although some of them left enigmatic drawings in stone, called petroglyphs, recorded history in Nevada began with the arrival of Spanish explorers in 1776. Considering the fact that the Spanish began exploring neighboring Arizona almost two hundred years earlier, you can perhaps grasp some of the intimidating power of the desert. Mexico won its independence from Spain in 1821 and among its prizes was the land that would become Nevada. Few were interested in exploration, development or settlement.

The United States took possession following the Mexican-American War of 1846-48. Mormon settlers began arriving in the 1850s. About that time silver was discovered around Virginia City and the rush was on. Thousands of miners poured into the state, followed quickly by more thousands of businesspeople who came to "mine the miners." Unlike most of Arizona, which favored the Confederacy, Nevadans favored the Union during the Civil War, joining in 1864. Carson City became the capital.

Following the war more silver was discovered as was gold and lead. Sheep and cattle ranches were founded. The Central Pacific Railroad allowed the state's goods to be shipped out to U.S. markets and for immigrants to be shipped in. Within less than 20 years the state's population grew from 15,000 to nearly 62,000. Unfortunately, the rollercoaster ride called the economy dipped in the 1880s when the mines played out and severe winters ruined many of the ranches. The population dwindled along with the fortunes of its inhabitants.

Things didn't bounce back until the turn of the century when new deposits of silver, copper and lead were discovered and irrigation made farming a practical occupation. The Great Depression hit Nevada hard, as it did all the states, but Nevada fought back. The state made gambling legal, an act that would eventually shape and reshape the fortunes of generations. Two other factors helped stabilize the economy. One was the building of Hoover Dam which created thousands of jobs in construction and in support businesses. The second factor was World War II which spurred mining and ranching to support the war effort.

Today, Nevada is the fastest growing state in the Union, a title it has earned since the 1960s. During the decade of 1990 – 2000 the state grew 66.3 percent and its present population is 2,106,074. Approximately 5,000 people *a month* move to Las Vegas alone. This population is highly concentrated. About 86 percent of the people live in or near cities and about 80 percent of those folks live in or near Las Vegas or Reno.

Nevada's Business

Service is king in Nevada, particularly in tourism and government. By far the largest sector of the economy is tourism which brings in about $33 billion a year. Most of this money, as you might guess, is spent at the casinos, resort hotels, ski resorts and the businesses that serve them such as restaurants and night clubs. The federal and state governments also employ thousands of people, many of them at Nellis Air Force Base near Las Vegas or in one of the state's parks and national forests.

Real estate is very big in Nevada and billions of dollars in property change hands every year. Commercial buildings, housing, and even raw land provide major opportunities for the investor. To say that Nevada is a "hot" market is to make an understatement of enormous proportions.

Mining still contributes to the economy and Nevada produces more gold and silver than any other of the United States. Copper and lead are still mined and oil has been discovered and drilled. Mining contributes about $3 billion to the economy each year.

Most of Nevada's manufacturing is centered on the cities of Las Vegas, Henderson, Reno and Carson City. Major goods produced include irrigation equipment, computer parts, chemicals and printed goods.

The advent of irrigation allowed productive use of very fertile soil. Farmers grow vegetables and fruits. Garlic and alfalfa seeds are important and hay is the number one crop in Nevada. Cattle, hogs and sheep are raised on approximately 2,500 ranches and farms.

Of course, you're aware of the gambling and entertainment Mecca that is Las Vegas, "the city that never sleeps." Although gambling was first introduced in Reno, Las Vegas quickly became the gambling capital of America. Recent years have seen a move toward more family-style entertainment, but the city will always relish and promote its "wicked" side.

Chapter Nine

Texas
"The Lone Star State"

Fact File:

Location: Southwestern United States bordered by Oklahoma to the north, Arkansas and Louisiana to the east, Mexico and the Gulf of Mexico to the south, and New Mexico to the west.

Population: 20,851,820

Size: 266,874 square miles

Capital City: Austin

Interstates: I-40, I-20 and I-10 run east/west; I-27 and I-35 run north/south.

Largest Cities: Dallas, Ft. Worth, El Paso, Austin, Houston, and San Antonio.

State Bird: Mockingbird

State Flower: Bluebonnet

State Tree: Pecan

State Song: "Texas, Our Texas"

State Shrub: Crape Myrtle

State Plant: Prickly-pear Cactus

State Mammal: Armadillo

State Flying Mammal: Mexican Free-tailed Bat

State Reptile: Horned Lizard

State Insect: Monarch Butterfly

State Fish: Guadaloupe Bass

State Shell: Lightning Whelk

State Pepper: Jalapeno

State Fruit: Texas Red Grapefruit

State Gem: Texas Blue Topaz

State Grass: Sideoats Gama

State Dish: Chili

State Fiber and Fabric: Cotton

State Sport: Rodeo

State Folk Dance: Square Dance

State Motto: Friendship

Admitted to the Union: December 29, 1845 as the 29th state.

The Texas Environment

Texas is big. What else would you expect from a state that has its own official whelk? Until Alaska was admitted, Texas was by far the biggest state in the Union. As befitting such a large land mass, the landscape and the environmental conditions are remarkably varied. A tourist beginning a drive west from East Texas would start out in hilly pine and cypress forests and even a few swamps. Dipping south he would encounter sandy beaches on the shores of the Gulf of Mexico. Moving westward he would drive through rolling hills, prairies and plains dotted with mesquite trees. Rugged mountains define the far southern Big Bend Country and the land northwestward toward El Paso. Sand dunes are in abundance around the small town of Monahans. The Great Plains are located in the northwest and are famous in western lore as the Llano Estacado, or "staked plains." Just south of the plains is a flat area called the Edwards Plateau. Many of its rivers are also famous in western legend and lore. Among them are the Red, Brazos, Trinity, Colorado, Canadian, Pecos and Rio Grande.

Wildlife is as varied as the landscape. Caddo Lake in the northeast is the state's largest and is noted for its cypress trees, hanging moss, and mysterious bayous and backwaters. Alligators are not commonly seen, but they're around. Coyotes, javalinas, armadillos, and deer populate the forests and swamps, as do numerous smaller mammals, amphibians and reptiles. The prairies and plains are covered with grasses and mesquite trees. Prairie dogs, armadillos, horned frogs and other wildlife survive well in this harsher climate. Dolphins and manatees are seen along the seacoast. Further west the land begins to take on the appearance of desert and desert mountains where mule deer and jackrabbits are common.

The Texas Gulf Coast is hot, humid and generally gets a good dowsing of rainfall throughout the year. Hurricanes can be a serious problem during the summer season. In the far northern "panhandle" section, snow and strong winds are common during the winters. Tornados are a regular feature of the central portion of the state. People in the Panhandle could be bundling up against a harsh wind and driving snow while at the same time people down in the Rio Grand Valley could be outdoors playing golf. As a general rule, if you want to experience a particular type of climate, you can find it somewhere in Texas.

Key Attractions

Austin is the state capital, so as you can imagine government is a big employer as is the University of Texas, which was founded here. If you're a fan of country western, bluegrass, contemporary country, rock 'n roll, blues, and other genres then your probably aware that the city bills itself as "the live music capital of the world." Live music is big business in this relatively small city.

Brownsville, on the Gulf of Mexico to the far south is an example of the close ties between U.S. communities and Mexico and her citizens. The city is economically and culturally tied to its sister city Matamoras across the border. Brownsville is a major seaport, railhead, and agricultural export center. Fortune 500 companies participate in the maquiladora (duel-frontier) manufacturing facilities. The city is also home to a large shrimping fleet.

Dallas is the very symbol of Texas to many people around the world, aided I'm sure by the enormously popular television series of the same name. There's really no reason for there to be a "Dallas" as we know it. The city isn't on a major river, the land isn't as fertile as other nearby areas, and there was just nothing to draw and hold people – except perhaps a dream. There's a Dallas, a legitimate major city, simply because the people there over time wanted it so. Today the once dusty little crossroad is one of the top ten largest cities in the U.S. and a commercial and financial giant.

The city is a major center for the oil and gas industry and it is rapidly becoming a center for high-technology manufacturing and innovation. Higher education is a big asset and a big business in Dallas. Institutions include Southern Methodist University, University of Texas at Dallas, University of Texas at Arlington, and other colleges and schools of higher learning.

Fort Worth is famous as a cattle town and justifiably so. Its stockyards are famous not only for their obvious use, but also as an entertainment center drawing tourists and locals who appreciate a touch of modern cowboy dining, dancing and music. The annual Fort Worth Stock Show and Rodeo brings in more than 850,000 people.

Forth Worth's economic base is broad enough to include defense contractors, high technology, aviation, and oil and gas.

Houston is a major metropolitan area and one of the country's largest and busiest seaports even though it's located 50 miles inland from the Gulf of Mexico. Energy is a major economic factor and includes oil and gas drilling, production, refining, and production of petrochemicals.

Other important industries are steel, synthetic rubber, chemicals and space exploration and related fields.

Houston is recognized around the world for the high quality of its medical care, making medicine and health care a major economic force. Higher education is another major economic factor. There are more than 25 institutions of higher learning, which include Rice University, Texas Southern University, Houston Baptist University, and the University of Texas.

El Paso is located in far Southwest Texas adjacent to New Mexico and on the Mexican border. Its sister city across the boarder is Ciudad Juarez. Major industries are agriculture, winter tourism, manufacturing, and the military at Ft. Bliss, home of the U.S. Army Defense System. *Midland-Odessa* are in the heart of Texas oil and gas production. *San Antonio* is home to the Alamo and a number of top universities and colleges. *Texarkana,* on the Texas and Arkansas state line has the only federal building, a post office, located in two states. And the small town of Seguin boasts the world's largest pecan. (It's a statue on the courthouse grounds.)

The Texas People

Paleo people roamed the land that would one day be called Texas, but the first true Texans were the Native Americans who established permanent dwellings or who lived a nomadic or semi-nomadic existence within its borders. Today three tribes are recognized. The Alabama-Coushatta live primarily on a reservation in northeast Texas. The Tigua live on the Ysleta del Sur Pueblo near El Paso in far west Texas. The Kickapoo live part of the year on their reservation near Eagle Pass and part of the year in Mexico. Free and unfettered travel back and forth is allowed by the governments of Mexico and the United States.

Hispanics have been part of the state's history since the arrival of the Spanish in 1528. Much of today's Hispanic population is comprised of immigrants from Mexico, although other Latin countries are well represented. African-Americans arrived during the years of slavery, the Civil War and the post war period. A small percentage of Asian-Americans make Texas their home, too. The population breakdown is: 52 percent white, 32 percent Hispanic, and 11 percent African-American. Many people of German, Czech and French ancestry live in the Texas Hill Country.

Most Texans who espouse religion are Christians. Approximately 3.5 million are Roman Catholics, the largest group, followed by Southern Baptists who have 3.3 million members. Other religions include the Greek Orthodox Church, the Lutherans, Conservative Baptists, and Jews.

Texas is one of the fastest growing states in the Union, making it an ideal locale for real estate investment. Almost four million people moved into the state during the decade of 1990 – 2000, making Texas the second most populous state after California. Three of the largest cities in America are in Texas: Houston, Dallas and San Antonio. The metro areas of McAllen/Edinburg/Mission, Austin/San Marcos, and Laredo were among the fastest growing metro areas during the 1990s. Each area grew more than 40 percent during that decade.

Texas History

Prehistoric Texas was populated by an amazing variety of Native American people. In East Texas the Caddo were members of the high-culture of mound builders. They farmed corn, beans and squash and had a trade network that extended into west Texas and perhaps as far as the New Mexican pueblos, up the Mississippi River and down into central Mexico. To the south were the Karonkawa, who were coastal dwellers, and the Coahuiltecs who were related, but lived inland. The Kiowa, Comanche, and Wichita tribes were primarily nomadic people on the plains. The Lipan Apaches roamed the Edwards Plateau. Other tribes were the Tonkawas of central Texas and the Jumanos of the southwest.

As you probably have guessed, the first Europeans in Texas were those adventurous Spaniards. Cabeza de Vaca was the first, although an unintentional explorer. He was the victim of a shipwreck near what would become Galveston. His seven-year journey as slave, runaway, and healer across Texas and finally down into settled Mexico is one of the great survival stories in western history.

Coronado passed through in 1541. The first Spanish mission was located near today's El Paso in 1682. Americans were invited to help settle Texas after Mexico won its independence from Spain. Taking a hint from their rulers, the "Texicans" soon won their own independence from Mexico in the 1830s. The famous battle of the Alamo was fought during this war.

The Republic of Texas ceased to exist in 1845 when Texas became the 29th of the United States. Mexico, which had never recognized the republic, declared war. The Mexican-American War lasted from 1846 – 1848 and ended with Mexico ceding territories that became all or parts of Texas, California, Utah, New Mexico and Arizona.

Texas seceded from the Union and was a member of the Confederacy during the Civil War. During and after Reconstruction, warfare continued, this time between red and white rather than the blue and the gray. The Indian wars continued for another decade. Much of the "cowboy" legend was developed during these years as inexpensive Texas cattle were herded in often-massive cattle drives to the northern railheads for shipment to mass markets to the east. Cattle ranching is still a major Texas industry.

The latter part of the 19th century saw much growth and progress in Texas, especially when the railroads linked its towns and cities to each other and to the rest of the country. Oil was discovered at the turn of the century. Later the state's largest oil field was discovered south of the Staked Plains and is know as the Permian Basin. A lot of modern Texas was financed by the oil and gas industry and the service and support industries that developed from it.

World War II brought new development as the state's military bases were activated. More than twelve new bases were created as were 40 airfields. More than 1.5 million soldiers and airmen were trained in Texas during the war years. Accelerated growth followed World War II. Even though the national and state economies rose and fell, overall Texas has remained a stable economic environment.

Texas Business

Texas contributes about $522 billion dollars a year to the U.S. economy and if the state were a country it would represent the 11th largest economy in the world. In the U.S. Texas ranks number three, behind California and New York. Texas also creates the second largest number of U.S. jobs per year.

The rich soils of southern and eastern Texas are ideal for growing crops and for raising cattle. "King Cotton" may not rule as it did in the days before the Civil War, but it is still a major crop. The state boasts millions of acres of good farmland which is put to good use growing oranges, grapefruits and winter vegetables, especially in the southern Rio Grand Valley. Other crops include corn, sorghum, hay, wheat, and rice.

About half the state's acreage is devoted to cattle ranching. Milk cows are raised in the northeast, beef cattle range the plains, and sheep herds can be found on the Edwards Plateau.

Texas is world-famous for its production of "black gold" – oil and some of the richest deposits in the world are here. Texas leads all other states in oil production, oil refining, and in cattle and cotton production, too.

Texans are not content to look to past glories or depend solely on them for economic stability and opportunity. Inventors such as Jack Kilby, who invented the computer chip, and Dr. Denton Cooley, who pioneered heart transplant surgery, did so in Texas. High tech industries are centered in Dallas and Austin. NASA moved its Mission Control and astronaut training programs to the Manned Space Flight Center (Johnson Space Center) near Houston in the early 1960s, further spurring the growth of high-tech industries. High-tech is so big in the Dallas Metro area that it is sometimes called "Silicon Prairie." Thanks to NAFTA, about one-third of all Texas exports are sold in Mexico and in 2001 Texas exported $52.2 billion to NAFTA countries. Service industries make up the largest segment of the economy. Major service industries include retail sales personnel, educators, medical practitioners and their service personnel, lawyers, tourism, and engineers who are prominent in the petrochemical, electronics and aerospace industries.

Chapter Ten

Secrets of the Wealthiest Americans

Of the 281,421,980 Americans recorded in the latest census, only an extremely small percentage qualified for that rare appellation "millionaire." As in any worthy human endeavor, only a dedicated few make it to the top. You can join that group and climb as high on the ladder as your energy and drive will allow. Yes, you can become wealthy, enormously wealthy. Use the magic found in real estate to make your fondest dreams come true.

I know what most of you are thinking. The financial drain of earning a living, supporting a family, paying off a mortgage, paying off a car note, saving money for college or retirement, and just providing basic food, clothing and shelter sometimes seems overwhelming. "How can I save enough money to invest in real estate when I'm struggling just to make ends meet?" I have never meant to imply that earning wealth is an easy task or that there aren't sacrifices. It's tough, but the result is well worth all the effort. Imagine yourself living a comfortable and secure life. Visualize yourself in a beautiful home surrounded by a happy family. See yourself watching your children graduate from college, traveling on exciting vacations in exotic places around the world, donating serious time and money to your favorite charity or cause, and you and your spouse enjoying a safe and secure retirement. All that and more is possible, especially if you choose the route provided by real estate.

Viewed in the proper context, wealth earned through real estate investing is the sensible route even for folks who believe they're too strapped for cash to invest. That's because:

1. There is so much real estate available throughout the country,

2. There is such variety of properties available that anyone's needs can be met,

3. *There are no prohibitive requirements for "regular Joes" to participate (degree, schooling, certifications, etc.)

4. There is such a wide range of pricing that virtually anyone can participate.

As far as I'm concerned, real estate is the surest way to (1) becoming a millionaire and of (2) making the next jump to the level of multi-millionaire.

The bull market of the 1990s wasn't a fluke. Markets come and go. We have good years and bad years, ups and downs, booms and busts. A lot of the financial problems investors experienced in 2000 – 2002 were a reflection of people's unwillingness to face this basic fact of life. People thought the stock market would be the best place to be for all time. Some politicians were promising an end to the business cycle. No more recessions. No more dips in the economy. Happy days are here again – and forever.

As Col. Potter on the television show M*A*S*H would say, "Horse hockey!" All good things come to an end. I'm not saying the stock market won't ever bounce back. It will. It has to, but it's not happening now and it's not likely to happen in a big way in the foreseeable future. Events during the first three years of this century proved how vulnerable owning stocks and mutual funds can be. Look up the statistics for yourself. As hard as it may be to believe, the majority of investors who placed all their emphasis on owning stocks and/or mutual funds have seen negative returns on their money throughout the past five to seven years. Many of them have had such problems for five to ten years.

Just think about that for a moment. Suppose someone had $200,000 invested in stocks and/or mutual funds in 1995 or 1996. After all these years, when that money should have been growing, the investor is worse off than ever. That $200,000 just isn't worth $200,000 anymore. The drops in the stock market, not to mention the ravages of inflation, have gutted that nest egg. We're not just talking dollars and cents here. That money represents a new home, a college education for the kids, vacation travel, financial and emotional rewards for decades of hard work, a safe and secure retirement, and more. But because all those eggs were placed in one basket, those dreams have to remain just that – dreams.

Saddest of all are the millions of investors who placed the bulk or even all of their funds in the hundreds and hundreds of companies in technology fields, companies that have completely folded and/or filed for bankruptcy. Many of these stocks were promoted as "hot" items by the so-called experts in the field. Maybe they were right at the time, but they weren't right for a very long time. Millions of people were unnecessarily burned. Add to that the scandal-ridden companies on the New York Stock Exchange that have devastated the finances and futures of their stockholders. The attack on investors' fortune by companies with names like Enron, WorldCom, Global Crossing, RiteAid, and so on will, like the attack on Pearl Harbor, "live in infamy." And they should. They earned it.

The best kept secret held by most millionaires is that they have invested virtually all of their money in real estate. Many of these millionaires have large holdings in a diversified portfolio that could include raw land, shopping centers, office buildings, apartments, houses, rental houses, industrial parks, parking garages, and so on. Others specialize in a limited area such as raw land. Many invest in first and second mortgages and trust deed investments secured by real estate. That's one of the beauties of this field. You can tailor your approach to your personal likes and dislikes. Your investments can be simple and focused or broad and complex and you can earn fantastic wealth either way.

* Of course, if you want degrees, certifications, and additional schooling, there are plenty of opportunities everywhere.

Chapter Eleven

Leverage – Your Quickest Way to Becoming a Multi-Millionaire

I promised to deliver the secrets of the wealthiest Americans in the last chapter and I will. It's just that the second big secret deserves a chapter all its own. *The biggest and most well-guarded secret used by the wealthy in virtually every transaction is the use of financial leverage.* Often it's just referred to as *leverage.* It is a way of conducting business by compounding your money and it is the quickest and best way to earn great wealth in real estate.

In its simplest terms, financial leverage is buying the largest amount of real estate you can with the least amount of down payment. It's a sound and proven way of doing business and it works equally well with raw land, housing, apartments, buildings, hotels, shopping centers, and any other real estate investment you'd care to name. Leverage – buying as much as you can with as little as you can.

Let's examine a few examples of leverage. Buying a house, something most of us have done or will do at least once in our lifetime, is a perfect example. Do you use your own money to buy a house? Of course not. You use OPM, Other People's Money, usually borrowed from a bank or savings and loan association. That's leverage. Why use your own assets when someone else's assets are readily available?

How does this philosophy translate into the world of real estate investment? Quite well, quite well indeed. Remember, in addition to living space, the home you purchase is also an investment vehicle. You already know how to do this. Here's an example of how leverage works on a small and easily-understood scale. Let's say you purchase a house for ten percent down, borrowing the other 90 percent from a financial institution. This is the way most people go about buying a home.

1. If the home is priced at $200,000, you pay $20,000 as your down payment and borrow the other $180,000 at five percent interest. A year later you are able to sell that house for $220,000. We'll assume in this and the following example that you didn't go through an agent and therefore didn't have to pay a commission on the sale. You only paid $20,000 down for the house so that means you made $20,000 on the sale – a 100 percent profit.

2. You didn't use leverage and instead paid $200,000 cash for the house. A year later you sell it for $220,000. You earn that same $20,000 as in the first example, *but because you didn't leverage your buy, your profit is only ten percent.*

Do you get my point? On the purchase made on terms, you made a 100 percent profit, but on the cash transaction, you only made a ten percent profit. The difference between the two is leverage and I think you'll agree that it's quite a difference. This, folks, is how you go about becoming a multi-millionaire. Yes, you had to pay interest on the purchase made on terms, but remember that the interest is tax deductible. There's another advantage to buying on terms. You then have money available to invest in other areas so that you can use financial leverage to earn even more money.

Again, we're assuming you didn't involve an agent and you deducted your interest payments from your taxes. Still, the biggest benefit to using leverage in example #1 is that you still have that $180,000 which can be used to make other financially-leveraged investments. It's more money piling up to make even more money. Real estate savvy investors know this and they've used it to become the wealthiest people in the world.

Financial leverage is absolutely the best way to compound your money. I know it from more than 40 years of personal experience. If you want to build true wealth, the opportunities to be found in Arizona, Florida, Nevada and Texas are nothing short of phenomenal. This is what you've been looking for. Take an example, raw land.

Cash payment of 100 acres of raw land
priced at $10,000 per acre
= $1,000,000.

Leveraging 100 acres of raw land
priced at $10,000 per acre (10% down)
= $100,000

Now let's allow a year to pass and you're able to sell that raw land for $11,000 per acre. If you're the cash buyer, you've earned a tidy profit of ten percent. If you're the smarter, more fortunate buyer who made the purchase using financial leverage, your profit is a whopping 100 percent! Both profits are nice, but the financial leveraged profit is a whole lot nicer, don't you think?

Of course, as with the purchase of the houses in the earlier examples, interest payments would be due. But these days interest rates are low and you could probably borrow the money at a rate of five percent. And again, think about all that money freed up for further investment when you use leveraging instead of paying cash for the full amount. This is the way people use leveraging to become millionaires. It's also the way millionaires compound their money to become multi-millionaires. Sounds like a plan to me!

Chapter Twelve

Raw Land
The Greatest Buy to Maximize Leverage

I feel a bit like one of those television announcers who used to provide the lead in from a program to a commercial with, "And now a few words from our sponsor." Well, real estate has sponsored great wealth for a great many people and I'm excited about sharing my experience and know-how on the subject. Before we get rolling and take a close look at specific areas of real estate investment, I'd like to offer a few words on why I think real estate is such a great vehicle for building wealth, security and peace of mind. And why it's so much darn fun! I've boiled down about 40 years of thinking on the subject into ten solid reasons. They apply across the board, so this seems like as good a place to share them as any. Raw land, and virtually any real estate property, offers you the real opportunity to enjoy the following ten benefits.

1. You control your assets. They're not left in the hands of a banker, investment counselor, stock broker, your "brother-in-law in the business," or some other person who may or may not have your best interests at heart. Controlling your own destiny can be intimidating, but if you're interested enough in real estate to purchase this book, you're probably the kind of person who likes the risks and rewards of calling his or her own shots.

2. Flexibility. You can pick and choose the area of real estate you are most comfortable with, which just gives you more control. You can work alone or with partners; deal with the public or with investors only; invest in buildings and structures in town or farms and ranches out of town; with individuals and families or business people; with industrial property, homes, retail space, empty space,

full space, or even "castles in the air" speculation, or a mix of all of the above and more. It's your choice.

3. Income. We all know that there's nothing guaranteed in life, but income from real estate comes pretty close. I've been buying, selling, renting, speculating in, winning and losing in real estate for four decades. Believe me, I wouldn't have hung around this long if I or my associates were losing money. Over the long haul, we've hauled in a lot of well-earned income and I don't see that trend changing in the foreseeable future.

4. Building equity. You can purchase a property and pay down your mortgage so that eventually you own a profitable business *debt free.* How's that for an incentive!

5. Appreciation of your assets. Like they say, land is always in demand because they're not making any more of it. Despite the ups and downs of the economy, real estate increases in value year after year after year. Few investments have that kind of track record for such a long period of time.

6. You can be your own boss. That's the nature of the entrepreneurial mind. Calling your own shots means you answer to yourself. If you answer to others, say your co-investors, that too is a matter of your own choice.

7. Creative challenges. As an owner of real estate you can "let your creative juices flow." Ownership offers wonderful challenges and opportunities to create something where nothing else or something else entirely has existed. Of course, that also opens the doorway to creating more wealth. Most folks see an empty lot or building and see only an eyesore. Real estate people see an office complex, a restaurant or retail outlet, a parking facility, a manufacturing plant, something that will create jobs, an economic base, an asset to the community – an opportunity.

8. Safety and security. I know the stock market is touted left and right and in all media. There are even a number of national television programs dedicated exclusively to the subject. I've watched and listened to them for years and can you guess the conclusion I've made? Real estate investments are significantly less volatile and safer. Period. That's all. End of discussion.

9. The sometimes radical ups and downs of the economies in other countries don't have the same impact on real estate as they do on stocks. Sure, there could be a negative impact, but nothing compared to the hits taken by the stock market.

10. CEOs, corporate presidents, board members, and other officers can in a remarkably short period of time turn a sound stock into a worthless piece of paper. You don't have that fear or that worry when you own real estate. The land, the building or the property is right *there*. You can always walk out and touch it. *You* can make improvements on it, enhance its value, market it, sell it and make a profit from it. The stuff is real.

Okay, let's get real about the specifics of real estate ownership, starting with raw land.

Raw Land is More than Dirt

Most people think of raw land as the dirt (rocks, trees, creeks, streams, hills, valleys and so on) located outside the city, town, or village. Raw land encompasses a good deal more. There are four broad categories.

Undeveloped land is probably what you visualized when you read "dirt" in the preceding paragraphs. This is land a good distance (a relative term, of course) from urban, suburban, or even small town development. It's "out there" far from the possibility of immediate development. Since there's not much happening out there, the opportunities for making a quick financial killing are limited at best. Then again, the Disney Company turned a bunch of undeveloped Florida swampland into some of the hottest real estate in the world. Careful shopping, even in the hinterland, can sometimes turn up a gold mine of opportunity.

Recreational land is generally where all those folks in campers, SUVs with recreational supplies strapped on top, and RVs with mud stains behind the wheels are headed late Friday afternoon. The possibility for rapid development of income is, with a few exceptions, rather limited. The lack of business activity at these locations is a chief reason behind so much activity on the weekends.

Agricultural land refers to farms and ranches. That's a tough way to make a living for the small, family operation. The larger concerns and commercial operations have their struggles, too. Currently in Arizona a lot of very big ranches have been broken up and are being sold in "ranchettes" of from ten to 40 acres. Even if there's little money in cattle, corn or cabbage, someone has obviously found a way to create income off the land.

Urban/suburban land is within the city and you'd be surprised how much undeveloped land can be found in cities, towns and villages. Since this is where most financial activity takes place, this is also where most of the real estate action takes place. Zoning permitting, there are so many different uses available for land that it's hard for the careful and wise investor not to make a profit.

With the exception of urban/suburban land (and even then there are exceptions), undeveloped land lacks the facilities we commonly take for granted in town: roads and streets, water and utilities, sewer systems, street lighting and so on.

Pros and Cons

Obviously, I'm a "pro" person. Otherwise the chapter title would probably have a subhead offering a dire warning such as "Keep Out!" or "No Trespassing!" Obviously, I don't feel that way. The rewards of purchasing raw land are not without risks, but to me the rewards are worth the effort. Let's take a balanced look.

On the con side there are a number of significant factors.

Raw land does not produce income. Yeah, you might find a reasonably priced piece of property containing oil and gas, gold or silver, or the Lost Dutchman Mine, but the odds are against you. Raw land is basically opportunity waiting to happen.

Your profitability curve may stretch over years, often a decade or more. That doesn't mean you can't make money. You can. Land that you can develop or resell faster will be closer to population centers and will therefore be more expensive. You'll turn your profit in less time. Land further out is less expensive, but will take longer to develop. You have to find the balance between how much you want to invest against how long you are willing to wait for that investment to pay off.

Initially, you may have to pay out a lot of money that you won't see back for a while. For example, your land may be ideal for one of those "ranchette" sites, but to close a sale you might have to drill a water well or make some other type of expensive improvement to the property. All of that is out go – not income.

Taxes are another consideration. They drain your bank account whether or not you're doing anything with your land. Big Brother always gets his cut even if it's just another slice of your dirt.

That being said, I'm very "pro" when it comes to purchasing raw land – the right raw land. There are a lot of benefits that to my mind far outweigh the disadvantages.

For example, comparatively speaking, raw land is very affordable. In many, many cases it's downright cheap.

Land that will some day become very expensive property is currently unused or underused and therefore not worth very much money – today. That's a real bargain for the right buyer who can afford the wait.

Raw land is a lot easier to buy than real estate in the middle of the city. There's just a whole lot less to deal with all around. For example, there's no municipality involved. The number of bureaucrats who can create delays and hassles is at a minimum. Your neighbors, the coyotes and ground squirrels, aren't likely to form a protest movement against your "exploitation" of the environment, community standards, or historical value of the property.

There's a lot of raw land around. This is especially true in Arizona, Florida, Nevada and Texas. These are big states covering a lot of territory and a lot of that territory is or can be for sale.

For people who buy right, the potential for making a profit is about as close to a sure thing as you can get. Look at how two key factors work to your advantage. (1) Nationwide, people are leaving the country and moving to the city. That means that land out there in the country loses value because fewer people are using it. The price drops, which is a good thing for the investor. (2) As people move to the city, the city expands. Land formerly "out there" becomes "close in." As the people move outward the price of that raw land increases, which is also good for the investor. The key, of course, is buying right.

How To Buy Raw Land

You can earn a profit off raw land any number of ways. Among them are: (1) buying land for purchase by a developer, or (2) become a developer, develop your land suitable for lots which you will sell to builders, and/or (3) become a builder and construct and sell homes on your land. Buyers can do just step one, one and two, or even all three. It all depends upon your financial situation, your areas of expertise, time frame, and willingness to take on a multitude of challenges. Some people go "whole hog" while others simply buy and sell the land and then start looking for more land elsewhere to buy and sell.

There are three basic steps to buying land right.

Step #1 is to select a general area (or areas) in which you want to purchase raw land. By general area I mean a large area such as southwestern Arizona, the Texas Panhandle, Florida's Gulf Coast, Nevada within 100 miles of Reno. You get the picture. At this stage of the game generalization is okay. If you don't like dust storms, you've eliminated the Texas panhandle and a good portion of Arizona and Nevada from your list. If you want to buy land by the sea, you've automatically narrowed your field to one side, Atlantic, of one state, Florida. Once you've done that you can move on. If you just want beautiful scenery, you can toss a dart at a map of any of the four states and come up a winner.

Step #2 is to analyze the direction of growth from municipalities within your target areas. For example, let's say you're interested in acquiring raw land near the mythical town of Moneda, Nevada. Land in the area is selling from a low of $500 an acre to $10,000 per acre. Now, all of it will appreciate and return a profit to its investors. Some will make a return in five to ten years while other properties will turn a substantial profit in five to ten months. Moneda is growing rapidly in all directions. Your task is to determine which path of growth is the most profitable.

How do you do that? It's pretty simple really. Get a basic map of the area or even draw your own. Study the market. Read the newspapers, the legal notices, advertising for new home construction, advertising of new retail or business centers, and any other pertinent news articles and features. Plot all these developments on your map. Over time, usually at least six months, you'll start to see a pattern or patterns of growth emerge. When that movement becomes obvious, you'll know in which direction to start shopping. That's not to say the other areas can't be productive. They can, but the real action will be found within the areas in which the city is growing.

Step #3 is to determine the speed of that growth. That speed will determine to a large extent the speed at which you have to acquire your raw land. This is pretty easy and simple to do. As you draw up your map, be sure to put dates beside each entry. There is a rule of thumb used in the real estate industry. A growing municipality moves outward from its center in the direction of growth at approximately one mile per year. If your land is five miles out, then the rule of thumb says you'll be at the edge of the city, and in a very profitable position, in about five years. Keep in mind that this is a very broad rule and that it may not, and probably will not, apply exactly to any given specific location. It's important that you conduct your own research to develop your own time frame based on information specific to your chosen area.

What to Look for in Raw Land

A Civil War general is said to have stated that victory belongs to him who "gets there firstest with the mostest." The phrasing is crude, but the sentiment is right on target.

There are many factors to evaluate in purchasing raw land. Chief among them is to get in on the deal as early as possible. That's how you earn the largest profits. Once development begins or often just the talk of development begins, land prices start rising. Land owners become less flexible. They want a lot more for their land than they did an hour before they read about the proposed industrial park or the arrival of Mr. Disney's people. Good timing on your purchase is essential. Perhaps we should amend the good general's comment to, "He that gets there firstest *makes* the mostest."

There are other factors and we've already looked at three of the most significant. Location is the most important consideration. The raw land you purchase must be in a location that will allow you to turn a profit. Some of the most beautiful land in the country can be had for little or nothing because nothing is happening or is planned to happen in, around, or near it. In other areas "worthless" swampland can quadruple in price overnight if someone sees those Disney folks driving the back roads.

Jobs, preferably long-term jobs, attract people – people who will want to buy land. A good climate is important, but don't neglect to consider man's ability to adapt to his climate. Phoenix and the Valley of the Sun have experienced explosive growth in only a few decades. Those decades followed immediately upon the introduction of available water and air conditioning, which turned the harsh desert into a paradise.

Other key factors include the availability or future availability of public services, such as utilities, sewerage lines, roads, police and fire protection, schools and such. The availability of nearby leisure time opportunities is important, especially in an era when individuals and families place a premium on "getting out." You'll find that some of the priciest land abuts state or federal land, where the views and recreational opportunities are close and aren't likely to change. Business and industrial development can be as lucrative for the land speculator as residential development. A small town may have 5,000 residents. A manufacturing plant may have just as many employees. All of them need a place to live, shop, and enjoy life and many will be in the market for land and homes.

You'll also need to evaluate conditions specific to your area. Earthquakes aren't a major concern in Texas or Florida, but tornados and hurricanes are serious and recurring events. We get an occasional tornado in Arizona and Nevada, but wildfires and flash floods are far more common problems. Private landowners hold a lot of the land back east, but here in the West governments and Indian nations control a staggering amount of the land. Your own financial situation, your personal resources, and your ability to borrow money are also factors. Past, present, and planned government uses for land are important. There is a chunk of raw land right in the middle of eventual growth patterns here in Arizona that I'd love to snap up. Unfortunately, it's within an artillery firing range and the ground is littered with decades of unexploded ammunition. That's not how I want to make a "big bang for my buck" in real estate.

Probably the easiest way for most investors to maximize their return with a portion of their investment capital is to purchase an interest in an LLC. You'll have to do your homework and closely evaluate the opportunities being offered in these four states. A truly good deal for one investor may not be a wise decision for another. Consider your income stream, your goals, your investment capital, your "fear factor" and the other important factors before investing in any opportunity.

Many highly qualified real estate people put an LLC together and offer membership interests to investors. You may need to call around to various real estate brokers and/or attorneys to see if they are aware of such investments. You are welcome to call us because we are always up-to-date on various LLC real estate opportunities. Our contact information is listed in the back of this book.

What do you look for in raw land? Everything. Look, examine and analyze every factor carefully. If you're buying for profit, leave your emotions behind. A beautiful view is fine if you're planning on retiring there in 20 years. If the location is in the middle of nowhere with no prospects of growth or development, that beautiful view may turn into an ugly picture. Keep your goals firmly in mind. Do your homework. And do your best to get there "firstest so you can make the mostest."

Chapter Thirteen

Homes and/or Condos
Your House "Rules"

In language that is popular as I'm writing this book, houses "rule," meaning that they're tops, the apex, or number one. By that I mean housing is the number one big investment common to most Americans. Although many think of housing primarily in terms of shelter, the purchase of a home is by any definition an investment. For the vast majority of buyers it has proven to be a wise investment. In some markets housing is so hot people have bought and sold at a tremendous profit houses that they never even had time to occupy. Unless you buy unwisely, and that can happen even in boom times, it's hard to avoid making a good investment in housing. You really have to work at failure.

I know, I know. You get a dose of negative economic woes from the news media every day. This is not the place to take a swipe at the nation's news organizations. Look at it this way. If 10,000 airplanes fly across the country safely and only one crashes, which flight are you going to cover? News, by its very nature often has to focus on the downside of life. Negative economic news will always out "pull" positive news. So what does this mean for the investor? You have to do a lot of economic research on your own. A lot of the good news, and there's plenty of it, will never make the nightly network, cable or local newscasts.

Here are a couple of examples of what's been going on in the last quarter of a century:

– More than 25 million U.S. jobs have been created,

– Our GDP (Gross Domestic Product) has risen from $2.7 trillion to almost $7 trillion,

- Exports have risen from $279 billion to about $700 billion,

- Virtually all positive economic conditions have been consistently on the upward swing, including population, income levels, exports, productivity, affordable housing, employment, GDP, and corporate profits,

- Virtually all negative economic conditions have been on a downward path, including unemployment, inflation, interest rates, and oil prices.

The bottom line here is that if you're an investor or if you're interested in investing, right now is a good time and right here is a good place – especially if right here is located in Arizona, Florida, Nevada or Texas. I'm optimistic on real estate in these areas. How can you lose? Well, it's possible...but you really have to work at it. Let's think in terms of winning and one of the best places to start is home or condominium ownership. I'll begin with traditional housing. To borrow a phrase, home is where the heart of investing is.

Buy to Rent

Buying a house as an investment is pretty basic and most of us do it without too much investigation into the return on investment area. We know it'll happen. We buy a house for $100,000, live in it a few years (let's say five), then sell it for $125,000, and use the profits to move up into a bigger and better house. But some folks look at a bigger and better financial picture. Suppose you bought a house for $100,000 and then rented it out at $2,000 per month. At the end of five years you'd have a house valued at $125,000 *and* you'd have an extra $120,000 rental income in the bank account. You could then sell the house, but your overall profit would be significantly higher. Or you could continue to rent the property, allowing its value to continue appreciating and continuing to earn a nice living from the rental. You might even consider buying other rental properties to increase that income. This is how many very successful real estate professionals begin a long and productive career.

That's where the real money is in buying rental properties. Buy them and rent them. Provided you buy right, there really isn't a down side to this plan and there are a lot of advantages.

Flexibility is a major advantage. You can purchase single-family dwellings, two-plex or four-plex housing, apartment buildings, or even apartment complexes. You're limited only by your imagination, current financial status (which continues to improve as you continue to invest), and the size of the task you're willing to take on. You don't have to be a multi-millionaire to "play the game" either. Lots of people on modest incomes have purchased small rental properties to turn that "modest" into "substantial" income. Many of the self-made real estate tycoons I know and have met began with a small investment in a small, single-family rental property. This is one of the fastest, easiest, and safest ways to begin building wealth through real estate.

Look at it this way. Most of us will buy a house anyway. Why not turn that house (and perhaps others) into a money maker?

There are other advantages. A steady cash flow heads the list. Even modest amounts of money from modest properties add up over time and give you the ability to increase your wealth by increasing your properties. Get this, please: not only do the investments pay for themselves, they fund other investments. An investor doesn't have to own Acme Deluxe Mega Towers in the high rent district to earn a substantial living in real estate. There's a lot of money, and I do mean a lot, to be made in older, less expensive properties that can be rented for moderate to high monthly payments. In other words, you don't have to be Donald Trump to think, act, buy, sell, rent and rake in the dough like "the Donald."

You really don't need a lot of management expertise for the smaller properties and professionals are always available when you move up to large properties. Maintenance and repair are financial, time, and customer satisfaction matters, but if you're a jack of all trades, you can handle most problems yourself. If you lack those skills or the time to handle those chores, you can make arrangements with any number of reliable individuals or companies to shoulder that burden.

If you have sound credit, financing is rarely a problem. As with any major purchase, you have to shop around, but I'm always coming across nothing-down and 100 percent financing real estate deals. Often a buyer can just assume the mortgage, that is, take up the payments on the property, and not have to put down one red cent up front. The opportunities are out there. If you look for them, you will find them. This is especially true in Arizona, Florida, Nevada and Texas where the continuing in-migration of people keeps the demand for property high.

The House Rules for Success

Every author/expert has his or her own set of guidelines for building wealth through owning residential rental property. They all boil down to six basic steps.

Step #1. Determine the type of property you want to own, rent and manage. Again, the market is wide open. You can choose anything from a single-family dwelling in a small neighborhood to an entire apartment complex in a downtown residential area. Obviously financial matters are important. How much is the down payment? The purchase price? Monthly utilities? Maintenance and repair? Taxes, insurances, and legal expenses? The unexpected?

What is your management expertise? Do you have the time even if you have the expertise? Can someone else handle the task better and more economically for you? What effect will changes in the economy have on your property? Is the neighborhood declining, stable or moving up? How stable is the area's economic base? Should you start small and learn as you go or jump in "whole hog?" You're the only one who can answer these questions, so I strongly urge you to give every aspect of your purchase in-depth consideration before you make any commitment.

Step #2. Determine how much you can invest in the project. It's probably less than you'd like, but more than you realize. A lot of available investment capital depends upon what the investors are willing to sacrifice to acquire and use it. Goals and sacrifice are twins. One follows the other as night to day.

I know of a young banking executive who bought and paid for a rather substantial house in 18 months. Everything he had went into paying that monthly note. He bought plain food in bulk at discount stores. He rode the city bus to work, took his vacation at home, and refrained from virtually any recreation that called for an expenditure of cash. He purchased only what he absolutely had to purchase. But at the end of a year and a half he had a beautiful house and no debt. More than that, all that monthly out-go could then be used to build wealth in other real estate ventures. He could at that point have bought another house and then paid down the mortgage from rental payments while soaking away a nice profit at the same time.

My experience has been that investment capital isn't so much a matter of having money. It's a matter of how available money is allocated. As I've indicated, I bet you have more money at your disposal than you think. Are you planning on buying a brand new car? Wouldn't a good used car be just as effective a mode of transportation? In fact, do you need a new mode of transportation at all? What about that big vacation? Couldn't you figure out an alternative that would allow you to bank some of those travel funds for investment purposes? Couldn't you get by just as well by foregoing your Saturday night on the town? Do you really (honestly now) need a satellite television, a home entertainment center, that new ski boat, new carpet, another dress suit, or the latest product or service just to "keep up with the Joneses?"

Really, a lot of potential investment dollars are readily available to you, even if you have to invest some time to save them up. It's really a matter of goals. Are you willing to sacrifice a few comforts today to build wealth for tomorrow?

Step #3. Find likely properties. This is a matter of personal research. Think of yourself as a detective on a case. Only instead of looking for a missing person, you're looking for a likely property. Start with the classified sections of the newspapers in your targeted area. Don't neglect the shoppers and neighborhood papers either. A lot of properties (opportunities) advertised there never make it to the larger-circulation dailies. These are great sources of real estate information, but they're not the only ones.

Banks, mortgage lenders, and municipalities can also be great sources of leads. A lot of viable properties have been abandoned by their owners or have been taken over by other entities because the owners no longer make payments. Generally, these organizations just want to get rid of the properties without losing a lot of time and money in the process. The buildings are more of a burden than anything else. You can often find amazing bargains from these sources.

Drive around your targeted areas. Look for "For Sale" signs. You'd be amazed at how many available properties are never listed in traditional, paid advertising media. Even on properties that are advertised, the signs often go up days before the ad reaches the public. You might be able to close a deal on a great property before anyone else even knows about it. Walk around the areas, too. A casual conversation with a resident, the postman, a route delivery person or even the regular patrol cop could easily lead to a home owner about to put his or her property on the market.

Opportunities are everywhere, but the sharp-eyed investor will seek out the best of the best. One great place to look is within neighborhoods that are just beginning to "bounce back." A lot of neighborhoods that have been rated bad because of economic blight, crime, lack of community involvement, or whatever become transitional neighborhoods. This means that they are in the process of making the transition from bad to good or even from terrible to great. The trick is to get in on the ground floor as early as possible so that you can take full advantage of the low prices. Often prices on such properties are phenomenally low.

When you believe you've found the right property, *have it professionally inspected.* I don't care how sound a property may appear, a pristine surface can hide a world of maintenance and repair nightmares. This is a job for the pros. They have the know-how, the experience and the tools to do the job right. A good inspector can often spot horrors during a cursory walk-through. You and I might never see those problems – until the complaints and repair bills started piling up.

A+B=C. You know what you want. It's out there. Go find it.

Step #4. Start buying. Notice that I didn't say buy the property. Buying is a process. I heard of some poor sap who always paid sticker price for his new cars – and bragged about it. He thought paying top dollar proved he was wealthy when all it did was prove what a remarkably poor business mind he had. Buying property is always a matter of negotiation. Never pay the "sticker price" for property.

The process is basic. The seller states a price. The buyer offers a lower price. The seller comes back with a slightly higher price, but one lower than the original. The buyer counter-offers and this game of financial ping-pong goes on until both parties agree upon a price. At that point it's really a matter of drawing up the legal documents, writing the checks and handing over the keys. Welcome to the world of rental property ownership.

Step #5. Get down to business. If you're inexperienced in owning and managing property, head down to the library or your nearest bookstore. You can find any number of excellent books on property management that will provide detailed instructions, recommendations, and even forms that you can use or adapt to your individual needs.

In general, you'll need to consider how you can fix up the property to attract higher paying, longer term renters. If you've done your homework (property inspections, etc.), the building is in sound shape and doesn't require major repairs or renovations. There are a lot of improvements you can make that (1) are very attractive to potential tenants and (2) don't really cost that much. A new paint job, new carpet, new fixtures, and similar cosmetic touch ups can really add significant value at a low cost. Wiring for cable television or putting up a satellite dish is another low-cost, high-value perk for your tenants. Look for and implement these opportunities.

Kitchens and bathrooms are what most people look at first and scrutinize the hardest when buying a new home. They're important for people looking at rental property, too. Fortunately, except for major repairs such as plumbing or wiring, you can do a lot without investing a lot. Look at your new property as if you were a renter rather than an owner. What would you like to see? What would keep you from renting? What would attract you? What could be added to enhance that attraction? Answer those questions, put a pencil to the matter, and if the numbers add up in your favor, make the changes. Happy tenants paying monthly rent will cover the additional costs in no time at all.

Step #6. Consider expanding your empire. If you can do it once, you can do it again. And what's wrong with having multiple income streams from multiple rental properties? Nothing at all. Just follow the initial five steps again (and again and again), being just as careful, just as wise and just as frugal. I think you'll be amazed at how quickly you can build you own empire and your own wealth through owning residential real estate.

Get Going on "Going Condo"

"Going condo" is a popular phrase for a popular form of real estate. The term refers to an apartment building converted into individual units that are purchased and owned instead of being rented. They are called condominiums or "condos." Actually, the owners purchase two very distinct properties: (1) the space in which they live, their "box of air," and (2) common areas (such as hallways, elevators, stairs, grounds, and so on) in which ownership is shared with the other owners in the building.

Condos offer a lot of advantages to the city dweller. He or she gets the benefits of home ownership, including tax advantages, ownership privileges, appreciation of an asset as real estate prices rise, and pride of ownership. These are combined with many of the benefits of apartment living. You can find and invest in or own all types of condos. Town house and apartment building styles are the most common and most popular, but you can also find office-building and even industrial-park condos. Again, real estate investing offers you a lot of flexibility and a lot of choice.

Condos are popular with investors for other reasons, too. For one, the investment is generally worth more than comparable properties because the space has a "higher use" capacity. There's more bang for the buck. Financing is often easier to arrange and 100 percent financing deals are not that hard to track down. The process of buying a condo, for living and/or for investing, is generally a bit faster and easier than for other types of real estate. When it's time to move out or move on, the demand for such quality properties generally means you can turn your property rather quickly. That means you can put those investment dollars back to work faster.

The process is similar to buying residential property. Decide what you want and where. Look for and find it. Negotiate and buy it. And start making money from it. Here's a brief overview of how it generally goes. We'll say that you've completed your shopping and have selected a property to purchase, an apartment building, for conversion to condominiums.

First you'll want to get the best possible mortgage for the new property. It's great if you can assume the existing mortgage – just take up the payments without a down payment or an increase in those payments. Determine if there are any second, third, fourth or other mortgages on the property. If you can't assume an existing mortgage, shop around for the best deal you can make on a new first mortgage to purchase the property.

Once you have the money, you can negotiate a contract to purchase the apartment building. This involves you (the buyer), the seller, attorneys, banks or mortgage lenders, real estate agents or brokers, and it's not a bad idea at all to run everything by your accountant or financial advisor. Once all the papers are signed, you are then the proud owner of an apartment building. Now you have to make the conversion.

It's not that difficult a process. After all, you're not rebuilding the building. You're just restructuring relation-ships. You'll need to contact your new tenants, the people who have been paying rent to the previous owner. Offer the right to become owners in the new property instead of just renters. Some will and some won't. But this is the logical starting point to find your buyers. These folks are already in place and for many of them the option of becoming an owner is the most logical, least costly over all, most financially astute, and easiest course to take. You can probably count on half or a bit more than half of the tenants to agree right away.

That's a great base. Get out the contracts and sign these new buyers up right away. You start out more than half your occupancy filled!

Now, before you start advertising for new buyers, start to work on the hold outs, those tenants who resist making the purchase. Chances are you can with a little extra work convert a good number of these folks from renters to buyers. One thing, you can point out that a lot of their neighbors have seen the wisdom of making just that move. The extra effort will pay off and you'll have a number of additional buyers. Only then do you need to promote your few remaining condos to the buying public.

Conversions to condos are popular and gaining in popularity all the time. If you think this area is your cup of tea, here are a few more basic tips.

- Use the fact that you're offering renters the opportunity of ownership and all the advantages that entails, including the tax advantages and appreciation of the value of *their* real estate.

- Look for the real bargains to purchase. A lot of owners leave the market for reasons out of their control, such as age, divorce, death in the family, ownership squabbles, a need for cash for other purposes. Their changing situation provides an opportunity for you to change yours.

- Until you get down to the technical and legal matters, deal buyer-to-owner if at all possible. There's less confusion and more real communication the fewer people involved.

- Do your homework. Know your own finances and financial resources. Get *all* the information about the property, including its financial status, the status of the owner, the building's physical condition, the nature of the neighborhood and community, the direction of the local economy, and so on before you commit to anything.

- Continually consult your lawyer, accountant, and banker throughout the process. Leave no area unexplored so you won't face any unpleasant surprises once you've signed the contract.

- Double check the local real estate market to make sure you're not overpaying for the property. Be careful if you discover that you're underpaying. If something looks too good to be true, it probably is. Watch out. Look at the advertising. Speak with real estate brokers, agents, and professionals. Don't be afraid to ask important questions.

- If some repair work is required, do it right away. If low cost, cosmetic changes will improve your chances, make those, too. Show the renters that you are serious about maintaining or even improving the facility and enhancing the value of their investment.

- Remember, a condo has to be managed. It's not like a house where you sell the property and walk away. If you're not the manager, you'll have to find someone or some organization to take care of that task for you.

- Carefully investigate your tenants and potential buyers before you sell. Think of your property as a living entity. You want everything to operate harmoniously. Good tenants make good neighbors and good business.

Chapter Fourteen

Hotels

As with any business venture or any investment, hotels and motels have their advantages and disadvantages. Hotels fall into the rather broad category of "special interests" which are related to, but quite different from the more traditional options that come to mind when we hear the phrase real estate investment. Naturally, there are significant risks. If you are in a position where you will have to personally manage or at least closely manage your hotel investment, you should make sure you have lots of time and energy. You should especially make sure you have the personality to deal with a demanding and often harsh pubic. There are also considerable rewards.

Many real estate experts advise against getting involved in the hotel-motel business. While I advise caution, as I would with any investment, I don't hesitate to recommend investing in the right hotel deal. I know from long, personal experience just how financially and personally rewarding the hotel business can be. So do the investors who joined me over the years.

Let's look at five key considerations.

1. Hotels are labor intensive. You need a lot of people to take care of a lot of other people: day managers, night managers, maids, maintenance and repair personnel, yard and pool men, and perhaps even cooks, bartenders and entertainers if you have a restaurant and/or bar.

2. Excellent management skills are required. Someone has to be able to work with, direct, entice, control, cajole and sometimes console. It's not at all like managing a staff or even a department of accountants, salespeople, other managers, or whomever where everyone pretty much does the same thing. A hotel

manager/owner doesn't have to know everything, but he or she sure has to be able to manage an incredible variety of people performing a wide variety of tasks. Of course, dealing with the public can present incredible challenges, too.

3. Hotels and motels can actually be several businesses within one business. You have the business of renting rooms to individuals, families and sometimes to groups and organizations. You could also have a restaurant from which these customers expect a certain level of food quality, beverage, and service. Speaking of beverage, you could also have a bar or even a nightclub associated with the property. This gets you into all kinds of legal areas, including regulation, zoning, fees, liabilities, unions, and insurance. These can be viewed as multiple headaches. Handled properly, the different businesses can be very profitable multiple-income streams. In fact, many hotels earn more money from restaurant and bar service than they do room rental.

4. The cost of land or land rental for hotels can be quite high. This makes sense. Hotels generally need to be on or near the best land, population centers, business and industrial areas, major traffic arteries and other conveniences and amenities. Naturally, prime locations come with prime prices. Even that lone oasis out in the Interstate wilderness, the only hotel within a hundred miles of civilization, is probably located on or near a major intersection or some feature that makes the property more expensive than the sagebrush and cactus studded desert around it.

5. Land values generally do not rise as fast for hotels and motels as they do for other forms of real estate.

Challenge and opportunity. They go hand-in-hand. It seems that the greatest opportunities are often accompanied by the requirement to overcome great challenges. That's certainly true in the hotel industry. It's not for everyone. But then again, no one investment is for everyone. Personally, my involvement in hotel/motel investing has proven to be extremely rewarding. Perhaps my experience, and the experience of the investors who joined me, will best illustrate my point.

"Landing" in Phoenix

My wife and I are among that fortunate group of people who have moved to one of the booming four states mentioned in the title of this book. We arrived in 1971 and quickly became involved in numerous real estate projects in Arizona. I met a transplanted Iowan named James Wirth who formed a company called Rare Earth Development Company for the primary purpose of land syndication. During the next four years more than 1,000 people bought into these land offerings. Business was good, the investors were happy, and I was fortunate enough to develop several hundred new clients. Virtually every investment realized great returns. Annual returns of 30 percent and higher were not uncommon. Moreover, several investors enjoyed returns exceeding 100 percent!

As if I really needed convincing, those years taught me that investment in quality real estate is an excellent way to build wealth and financial security. Keep that in mind, please, as you read through this book. The information I'm passing along isn't "book 'learnin.'" It's based on real-world, tried-and-true, personal experience. I know it because I've done it. Those early days led from one success to another and in 1975 I met a gentleman by the name of Robert Woolley, a man with a new and staggeringly brilliant real estate concept.

A Suite Deal

Bob is the recognized pioneer of the all-suite hotel concept. Sure, all-suite hotels are now a common feature of our cities and highways. But 30 years ago, suites were basically available to the high-rollers in the more expensive hotels in larger cities. Bob brought the concept into the world of the middle-class business and family traveler. His brainchild was called the Granada Royale Hometel. His concept provided guests with hotel suites, a full free breakfast, and a two-hour cocktail party in the early evening. That was revolutionary thinking back in the seventies and Bob was the talk of the hotel industry.

He wanted to expand. He wanted to build a large chain and that required a large number of investors who could participate in individual hotel partnerships. That's where I came in. I became part of the project to draw up the financial plan and to raise the majority of the capital. The first hotel opened in Tucson, AZ in 1975. Our second offering was the Granada Royale Hometel in Phoenix in 1976. Both investments paid fantastic returns very quickly.

We kept making new offerings throughout the country: Minneapolis, MN and Buena Park, Downey, Covina, and Arcadia-Pasadena in California. The public responded and the chain continued growing.

Bob's all-suite hotel concept began to make inroads into the business of the larger hotel chains as more and more customers responded positively to the features, benefits and services our chain provided. We were making waves and had become the hottest thing in the business. We were also returning terrific profits to our investors.

The years 1975 – 1984 were years of expansion, excitement and profitability as we charted new courses through new business waters. Nearly a decade after we started, Embassy Suites purchased all of the Granada Royale Hometels, the franchise Company, and the management company from Bob Woolley for the rather substantial sum of $111 million. Bob was a young man, still in his forties, and he wasn't about to retire. Even though he became a very wealthy man, Bob Woolley loved the hotel business and he kept on building larger and more beautiful hotels. He decided to continue building all-suites hotels as an Embassy Suites franchise owner. We kept on doing just what we did for Granada Royale Hometels and raised the necessary equity to build ten more Embassy Suites hotels. As I write this book, Embassy Suites is recognized as the leader in upscale all-suites hotels and it all started because of the vision, dedication, and determination of Bob Woolley to change the face of the hotel industry.

I think you can see why I'm so bullish on hotel/motel investments, especially in the growing markets of Arizona, Florida, Nevada and Texas. I've seen and participated in the making of real estate fortunes for brilliant business leaders, business people such as myself, and for thousands of investors just like you.

Chapter Fifteen

Apartments

After personal home ownership, the next step most real estate investors take is owning and renting residential property. Some remain in that market. Others use the gained experience and capital as a springboard to a legitimate empire in residential and other real estate areas. If you've never invested in real estate before, other than perhaps your own home, this is an excellent way to test the waters and get your feet wet. The leap from owning and managing a single-unit or four-plex unit to small apartment buildings or complexes isn't all that different or that much more challenging. In other words, you can build that empire, if that's your plan, one basic and doable step at a time.

Demand for Apartments Remains Strong

Certain segments of the population are drawn to apartment living and they always will be. Students are a mainstay of the real estate economy in college towns. Young adults entering the job markets, young singles, and young married couples, almost always live in apartments before purchasing their first house. Even established married couples with children often put off buying a home and remain apartment dwellers for some time. Older people and retirees are often attracted to apartments because they no longer need a large house for the kids, they're tired of the hassles associated with home ownership, they desire a simpler life, or they want to invest their money in areas other than house payments. There's a big market out there, several of them actually, and that market will remain strong.

While the suburbs continue to grow, always a good market, too, there has during the past half century seen a resurgence in urban living. Apartments have been a major factor in that change of direction. Not everyone is cut out for

116

the suburban lifestyle of lawns, backyard fences and weekend bar-b-cues. A lot of folks really don't care for watering and mowing a lawn, keeping up the interior and exterior of a house, and dealing with the wide variety of zoning, taxes and even neighborhood housing restrictions forced on many home owners. Apartment living is much simpler.

A lot of people prefer apartment living because all those watering, mowing, fixing up and repairing chores are handled by someone else. They prefer living closer to the cultural, entertainment, and civic opportunities found in the urban areas of a community. Let's face it, suburban areas have those too, but you'll find a significantly higher concentration of arts, entertainment, culture, politics, and so on within the urban areas than you will in the suburban ones. Many of the urban neighborhoods that bottomed out during the past decades, the areas that sent many people fleeing the city in the first place, are making a strong comeback. A lot of urban-oriented folks are making a comeback of their own.

There's another factor to consider and it's one of the prime reasons for investing in real estate: the supply of land is limited. Urbanization is devouring the landscape around our cities. Sometimes the movement is amazingly fast. As people lose the opportunity to move out, they start moving up. Instead of building houses outward on different parcels of land, it becomes much more feasible to build those houses, called apartments, on top of each other. As land becomes more valuable, people have to make more and better use of it. Why tie up land for a single family of four in a one-story home, when you can provide a home for dozens of families in a multi-story apartment building? It just makes good sense economically, environmentally, and, for the investor, financially. All these factors, and others, strongly suggest a long and stable financial future for those folks who purchase apartment buildings.

Stay Close to Home

There are exceptions, there are always exceptions, but generally the apartment building you purchase should be located within an hour's drive of your office. A half-hour's drive is even better. Why? As an owner you are going to get calls from your tenants and some of those calls will have to be answered in person. If you are an owner/manager you will get a lot more calls and if you're an owner/manager/repairman the calls will be virtually constant. It's one thing to drive a few minutes out of your way after work to pour oil on the trouble waters brewing in Apartment 3B. That's no big deal and it's always in your interest to go the extra mile to keep your tenants happy. It's another matter altogether when you have to leave home at midnight and drive a couple of hours just to tighten a loose pipe fitting, find out why the electricity is out, or referee a dispute between a couple of angry tenants. The trials and tribulations of distance increase dramatically as the severity of the problem escalates. Gamblers always keep things "close to the vest" and that's a good rule for property owner/managers.

Conduct Serious Research

There's always a deal. The thing is, you want to find the best possible deal and that requires a substantial investment in time, energy and resources. Find your apartment building using the same techniques used to find a house:

- read the classifieds

- drive around

- inquire about For Sale signs

- talk to people in the neighborhood

- network with real estate professionals

Look at three key factors with particular interest: employment, recreation, and transportation. Jobs, as you've already read here, are key to attracting and holding a population base to a state, city, community, or even a neighborhood. Is there a sound economic base in your target community and is it likely to remain sound for the number of years you need to assure your investment pays off? You don't necessarily want to purchase an apartment building right next door to the Horse Entrails Rendering Plant #3, but you do want to be in close proximity to good jobs for your tenants. Ideally, there will be a broad base of employment in the area. A good rule of thumb is to seek out properties that are within a half hour or less travel time of good, stable employment.

Transportation is also important. People have to be able to get to and from all those jobs that provide the money to pay all that monthly rent. Low income tenants need ready access to public transportation. Middle and upper income tenants who drive cars need ready access to major traffic arteries. Access to a park-n-ride facility set up with the city bus system, which combines both options, is a plus.

Recreation is a major consideration, especially in urban areas where it's more difficult for mom, pop and the kids to head out to the woods, river or area lake on a Sunday afternoon. Most people, even the overworked and workaholics, still find some leisure time and they need outlets. City parks, regional parks, golf and tennis courses, ball fields, and jogging tracks are plusses. So are museums and galleries, historical sites, and areas set aside for carnivals and festivals. Consider everything in terms of how the amenities meet or don't meet the needs of the people who are and will be your tenants. A great senior center is an asset to any community, but it won't do much to attract college students or young married couples. Nearby nightclubs featuring rock bands with names like "Guns 'N Spit" could be a plus for younger tenants, but to older renters who prefer the Dave Brubeck Quartet or the ballads of Miles Davis might look in another neighborhood and at another apartment. What's good for your people is good for your business.

Don't be intimidated by apartment buildings you think might be too big or too complex to handle, especially if you're just starting out. Earning money through apartment buildings requires thinking in terms of multiples and there are wonderful economies in having a lot of tenants. Don't limit your search to buildings with 15 or less units just because you think you can't handle one with 30 units. Here's an example. Suppose your yard maintenance and upkeep expenses run $200 a month. You need the tenants to pay for that amount so they can continue to enjoy the benefits of a neat and clean environment. With just ten tenants, you have to bump your monthly rates by $20 to absorb the cost. A rate increase of that size will surely be noticed by sharp renters who comparison shop. Now, if you have 30 tenants, you can bump the rate by less than seven dollars each, a figure that's much easier for each tenant to absorb.

Please invest sufficient time. A year is not too much if at the end of that period you have found an ideal property. Once you have found what you believe to be the right property, it is essential that you meet the existing tenants. They're the ones living in the building 24/7 and they're the ones who know the good features and benefits...and where the nightmares might be hidden. Also, you'll probably want to hold on to most of these folks. Good, reliable tenants are (literally) a gold mine. It's a good idea to start building solid relationships as early as possible.

Evaluate What You've Found

Traditionally, neighborhoods pass through three phases. Although the dividing lines between phases are often murky and the transitions can take place over decades, the phases themselves are quite distinct. They are:

Phase #1. Development

Phase #2. Growth

Phase #3. Decline

Fortunately, in many areas a fourth phase has been or is being added these days.

Phase #4. Rejuvenation.

I'm not saying that all four phases are bad or good. There is money to be made or lost in each one, but some are definitely more positive than the others. Your goal is to buy in at the right time. Early in the growth phase, for example, is good because you'll find lots of undeveloped property selling for reasonable prices. As the community grows, so do your property values. These can, of course, decline when the neighborhood slips from growth into decline. Money can still be made in a declining area, but you will probably face a lot of headaches associated with such neighborhoods. These could include a high crime rate, social problems, and renters who are difficult to work with. As I've said, many of these troubled neighborhoods are bouncing back and many a former eye-sore is now a very high-priced piece of real estate. Buying property in the declining phase just before rejuvenation hits is, clearly, a great buy.

The point is basic. You really have to know what and where you're buying. Walk the streets. Talk to people. Compare buildings and prices. Find out how people think of their neighborhood. Do they even think of it as a neighborhood? Get a good feel for the area and the people. What do they need from an apartment, an apartment building, and apartment management? What can and what should you provide? Is it worth your investment to provide those things? Can you improve the look and therefore the rentals of a property with relatively inexpensive cosmetic changes or will you be required to make substantial and expensive renovations? Can you earn your money back? How quickly?

Ask all the questions you can think of and work hard on the answers.

Can You Make Money Here?

Obviously, this is a critical question and its answer requires critical thinking on your part. How much can you earn from this property and is that enough? Let's say the building you want to purchase has 15 units which are being rented at $350 each month for a total monthly total of $5250 or $63,000 yearly. Watch out for the seller who tells you what the apartments "ought" to be rented for. "You can easily charge twice that amount" sounds great, but you'd be foolish to make a deal without conducting some of your own research. What if comparable buildings in the neighborhood are being rented for $250 - $300 a month? How competitive can you really hope to be? Won't you have to lower your rates? How will that shift affect your net income? Be sure to note which phase the neighborhood is in and which way the rental rates are moving. Are they getting higher or are they falling?

Check out the vacancy rates for the entire neighborhood. Lot's of vacancies mean lots of competition. Full or nearly full occupancy means there's a lot of competition for good space and rates should be at a premium. Don't let the fact that the building you're evaluating has a low occupancy rate, even if that rate is 50 percent. That's not necessarily a problem. A change in management, a few cosmetic touch ups, genuine marketing, and perhaps a little one-on-one friendliness have been known to turn around many a sinking real estate venture.

When buying an existing property, get a look at the books. Look carefully at the operating expenses. Look for any problem areas that might indicate major problems in place or developing. Are there a lot of water damage repairs, for example? Has the owner been patching a lot of pipes hoping to sell out before the damn bursts? Note how promptly the tenants pay their rent and pay particular attention to problem tenants. Look at the complaint log, repair bills, maintenance costs, city inspections, and so on.

Get a firm handle on all, and I do mean all, of the costs associated with operating that building: maintenance, repair, utilities, equipment purchases, garbage collection, grounds upkeep, taxes, insurance, legal, cost of borrowing money, management, accounting, advertising and promotion, tenant perks (such as parties, newsletters, and so on) anything and everything. Be sure to get figures covering several years so that you get an accurate picture of the property's performance over time.

Are you going to be an owner/manager or an absentee owner? If you choose the latter, then you'll need to hire a manager and set up and staff an office, even if the manager represents 100 percent of the management staff. Even if he or she works out of an apartment you rent at a reduced rate (a pretty good option for all involved), there are still regular office expenses.

Calculate your gross income. In our example, assuming you rent all units at top dollar, we've calculated that figure at $63,000. Now deduct your estimated costs. This gives you your net income. If you have to invest $70,000 to earn $63,000, something's got to give. More likely, someone has to move on to another investment opportunity. Estimate what would be the impact if some of your tenants left. How long can you operate with less than 100 percent occupancy? It is important that you be absolutely honest with yourself before you make the financial commitment. There are always good apartment building deals out there. If the one you're looking at doesn't really work out, relax. You'll find another one soon that is a better match for your needs...and your financial situation.

I pass along a number of "rule of thumb" guidelines in this book. They're handy, but they're not absolute. You must evaluate every situation and every rule of thumb in very realistic terms that relate directly to your specific situation. That being said, here's another. The rule of thumb says that total expenses should run no more than 30 percent to 40 percent of actual income. You should be able to meet your mortgage debt service with 50 percent or less of your income from your property. Again, those aren't cold hard facts. There just a general guideline, but in most cases they'll hold true to form. If your operations aren't running better or pretty close to those figures, something's probably out of whack. See that your financial picture doesn't get "whacked" by whatever that may be.

The bottom line is that investing in apartments requires a lot of work, time, energy and expense. It's an area that's not right for everyone, especially those folks who do not like to work with the public. But, for many investors apartments are ideal. A good property with good tenants in a good neighborhood is a wonderful source of income month after month and year after year. Best of all, the demand is strong and it looks like that's an equally strong, continuing trend.

Chapter Sixteen

Offices

When you drive through a city of any size one of the dominant traits of the downtown area will be a series of high-rise office buildings. That's the type of structure most people picture when they think of "downtown." Those buildings are well and good and if they're managed well the financial returns can be very good indeed. But those large, complex buildings are in a different and unapproachable league for most investors. That doesn't mean most of us are shut out of the game. The next time you drive through a downtown, look at what surrounds those high rise office complexes – smaller offices, lots of smaller offices.

American business is by far *small* business and all those business people need someplace to hang their business hats. Owners and managers need land, buildings, reception areas, show rooms, storage areas, parking spaces, utilities and reliable real estate providers to help them run an efficient and profitable operation. You can build a sizeable real estate fortune by helping other business people earn their own fortunes.

There's a real market opportunity that's just about open to any investor. And one of the best factors is that the need for office space isn't limited to the pricey downtown areas. Suburban areas, shopping centers, small cities, towns and even villages have needs for offices and that means there's an incredible variety of opportunity for the savvy real estate investor. Regardless of the type of business, occupants of the high-rise office buildings are pretty much all, well, office types. Small business has an incredibly broader set of needs. Look around at the variety of businesses and business opportunities you can support: gasoline stations, pizza parlors, flower shops, employment agencies, beauty salons, television movie rental outlets, doctors and dentists offices, clothing stores, and so much more. The business applications and the real estate opportunities are limitless.

One of the real advantages associated with office building ownership and management is the fact that it's simpler and more efficient when compared to residential real estate. For example, tenant ordinances and tenant's bill of rights policies generally don't apply to commercial enterprises. I'm not necessarily against those policies. It's just that life is simpler when you don't have to deal with them. Municipalities generally seem to think that people in business have the ability or should have the ability to look after their own interests better than the "just folks" renting living space in the same communities.

Since you'll be dealing with business types, chances are you'll be dealing with people who can plan, organize and manage a business, which generally makes the landlord's job a bit easier. Believe me, this isn't always the case, but the averages are better than when renting living space. There are other benefits. You can often structure your contracts so that your tenants are responsible for part or even all of their utilities, repairs, maintenance expenses, insurance and taxes. In most cases you'll experience a lot more flexibility when renting offices than when renting housing. Owner/landlords and tenants seem to like things that way because both sides tend to benefit.

There are important financial considerations you should be aware of and these can vary significantly from community to community and even from neighborhood to neighborhood. For instance, you'll probably need more upfront cash and equity in order to purchase commercial properties. I've found that pretty much across the board equity payments for commercial properties are 20 – 35 percent, compared to just 20 percent for multi-tenant apartments. Well, that's just the cost of doing business. What you have to focus your attention on is the profit to be obtained from conducting that business.

If you're new to commercial real estate, I highly recommend that you start out small. Develop your know-how, skills, and experience with a small, multi-tenant complex that provides the beginner with a little leeway for making beginner's errors. Don't worry. Such properties are everywhere and in every locality. Just drive around your own neighborhood with an eye out for office real estate and you'll probably be surprised at the amount and variety of opportunity you've never really noticed previously.

Multi-tenant properties mean that you can structure your business so that you're not dependant upon a single source of income. Ideally, you should arrange things so that you remain financially sound and profitable even if some of your space remains empty for a time. The income from other tenants should be able to cover your bank note, utilities, insurance, taxes and other expenses until the space is rented out again. Remember, things change. The neighborhood could start to deteriorate, the economy could turn sour, you could experience an unexpected catastrophe, or any number of events could affect the profitability of your office rentals. Hope for the best, but always plan for the worst.

As I've noted, generally business people have the capacity to plan and organize which *can* make the landlord's life much easier. Still, there are those business people who are inept, dishonest, or just plain unlucky. Don't allow their problems to become your problems.

One of the best ways to avoid serious problems is to run a credit check on every potential tenant. Don't be shy about it either. You're not questioning someone's ethics, accusing them of being bad business people, or implying anything negative at all. You're just taking care of business the way a businessperson should. This is a responsibility every owner/landlord should take seriously. To fall prey to a false sense of guilt or a potential tenant's sob story is to create problems down the road you do not want to face.

Check their credit rating. Get their Dun & Bradstreet rating, bank statements, accounts receivable, credit history, references from previous landlords, and any other documentation you feel justified. Be sure to check with your lawyer to make sure that you comply with the appropriate privacy rules and regulations for your area. There's always a "line in the sand" and a good real estate professional knows how to get the information he or she needs without crossing it.

As with any wealth-building plan, I believe it is imperative that the investor diversify. That's certainly true when it comes to office buildings. They are more susceptible to the ups and downs of the economy than other properties, certainly more so than housing rentals.

It's important to see things from your tenants' viewpoint. No matter how happy they may be, they'll most likely think of your office as only a temporary place in which to do business. To you it's a long-term investment. To them it's just a place between "there" and "over yonder." If the economy takes a nosedive, it's much easier financially, and certainly emotionally, for tenants to leave a building than for the owner to lose that business.

You need look no further than the effects of the stock market downturn of the first three years of this century to find thousands of examples. A lot of owners and landlords found themselves with a lot of very empty space as large companies began downsizing, reducing inventories, cutting suppliers and reducing costs. Those cuts filtered down and throughout the business community.

Yet many, many people in real estate sailed right through the crisis. Perhaps they experienced a bit of turbulence here and there, but they made it through and even prospered. Their secret?

Diversification is the key. Purchase different types of properties and rent to different types of businesses and industries. There's a business adage that is most certainly true when applied to real estate. One man's loss is another man's gain. When the economy, or whatever, hammers one type of business another type of business will prosper for the same reason. If housing sales are slow, apartment rentals will be active. If new car sales are down, business on the used car lot will be up. That's just a rule of business. A smart real estate pro knows that and structures his or her business to account for it.

Diversify. Diversify, ride out the storms, and sail into a safe harbor of prosperity.

Chapter Seventeen

Retail Stores and Shopping Centers

People buy things. They just love to buy things. In fact, in some areas shopping is practically a form of recreation or a means of entertainment. People also like convenient shopping. They'd rather drive to the mall or shopping center to visit dozens of shops in one location than make a dozen drives to visit the same variety of shops scattered all across town. As long as there are human beings we will have retail business and that trait will always drive a need for retail space – real estate.

You'll need to evaluate a number of factors before making your decision as to which retail store or which shopping center to purchase. Let's take a quick look at the most important ones.

Location...Location...Location

It's an overused adage, but it's a proven one. The three most important factors in the success of a retail business are location, location, and location. You've heard it, but it's important that you believe it and operate on it. What, then, does "location" actually mean?

Poor locations mean poor business – poor business for your tenant(s) which translates directly into poor business for the real estate investor. When it comes to selecting a location for a business or for selecting an existing business to purchase, don't be penny wise and pound foolish. Of course the poorer locations require less investment. You can pick up land and buildings for much less money. But are you really saving anything? The costs of putting up a building are the same in good locations as they are in bad locations. The price of electricity, gas, water, sewerage, lumber, fixtures, computers, letterhead, pencils, postage stamps and so on is just the same for a good location as for a bad one.

Therefore, a key factor is the value of the land. A poor location will require a much higher percentage of your overhead than a good location because you or your tenant just can't do enough volume business to compensate for the lack of traffic in a poor location. In other words you have to conduct a lot more business just to approach breaking even.

A good location pays for itself, especially when compared to the woes associated with a poor one. Another location-related factor is the type of tenant attracted to good locations – good ones. A business savvy tenant looks for a good location because he or she knows the importance of location to the success of a business. You want smart tenants. The better they do, the better you do. Also, word gets around. Once it's known in the business community that you are an investor who carefully selects good locations, you'll find other savvy retail merchants following your lead, ready and willing to sign up at your latest good location.

Retail stores often feature loss leaders, items sold at a discount, at cost or sometimes even at a loss because the owners know that the lower prices will bring in more customers. Shopping center owners do something along the same lines. One factor that draws people to a store is its proximity to other stores at which the customer(s) like to shop or would like to try. One of the reasons I go to the shoe store at X&Y streets is because there's a clothing store, a drugstore, and a place to get a hamburger for lunch at the same location. I, and many other people, place a premium on my time and the more convenient the shopping experience, the more likely I will be to patronize stores at such a location.

Shopping center or mall owners often provide space to large department stores at a reduced per-square-foot rate for the same reason. They know that a Sears or a J.C. Penny "anchor" in the facility will automatically draw a lot of customers for the other stores. That's why the owners of the smaller stores don't raise heck at the disparity of space rates. They realize that the situation creates a win/win proposition for all involved. Some tenants will tie their success so closely with the availability of a nearby anchor that they'll insist on a leasing clause allowing them to cancel that lease should the anchor move out of the center.

They say that variety is the spice of life. That's true. It's equally true that variety is the spice of retail business.

Physical Plant

Of primary concern is the size and shape of the property you're considering for purchase. Happy tenants can become raging demons when complaining about water leaks, falling ceilings, non-functioning appliances, failing utilities, broken fixtures, and…well, you name it and they'll complain about it. It's no fun paying for those landlord responsibilities either. Make sure your property is in good shape. Inspection by a knowledgeable and experienced professional is essential. Conduct at least two inspections. The initial inspection can be somewhat cursory, as you're still weeding the wheat from the chaff. The second had better be conducted with the proverbial fine toothed comb. The things you miss up front end up being the things you pay for down the road.

Make sure the physical layout is convenient for customers as well as for your tenants. Note how much flexibility you have in making changes to meet the requirements of new tenants. Are there good sight lines? That is, can customers see the stores (and store signage) well? Will the customers be comfortable? Will their shopping experience be a pleasant one? Does the parking lot flood? Is there enough security lighting in the parking lot? Can you afford to maintain the cosmetic appearance of the facility and grounds?

If you're looking into the purchase of a shopping center, there are three basic types of facilities. *Regional* shopping centers are those huge facilities drawing from a large population base located within seven to ten miles. Large, national anchor stores are a major feature as are an amazing and sometimes constantly changing number of stores. The anchor store(s) may occupy 100,000 to 200,000 sq. ft. by itself. If you can think of it and if it is in popular demand, you'll probably find what you're looking for in one of these centers. They usually require a population base of 400,000 to 500,000 to survive.

Community shopping centers serve a smaller area and population base, usually about 45,000 to 50,000 people located within a five-mile circle of the center. A popular retail outlet such as a Sears or J.C. Penny store often serves as the anchor. The variety of stores and shopping opportunities are quite broad and are geared primarily to middle-class buyers.

Neighborhood shopping centers feature retail stores catering to the basic needs of people in the immediate vicinity. A population base of 10,000 people is considered necessary for business success. Usually the anchor store is a grocery store occupying 20,000 to 25,000 sq. ft. The center will have less variety and specialized shopping opportunities than a community center because there is a smaller population base from which to draw.

Driving and Parking

Another key factor in selecting a location is its accessibility by automobile. We are for the most part an automobile driven society. Pardon the pun, but it's true. A good location is one that (1) can be easily reached by car and (2) has access to plenty of convenient parking for those cars. This means that major traffic arteries should be close by. Access to your property shouldn't be blocked by traffic medians or poorly designed streets. Through traffic shouldn't be a hindrance to local traffic. People should be able to turn from the street quickly and easily into your parking lot or the nearby parking area. The harder it is for customers to drive into your facility, the easier it is for them to drive on to another.

How much parking space is available within 150 – 250 feet of the store or shopping center you're considering? It's important because of one of those rules of thumb I keep feeding you. People like to drive to do their shopping, but they don't like to carry packages long distances from a store to their car. About 250 feet is the limit of their patience, willingness and shoe leather. In some areas there's also a concern for security, especially at night or during the holidays. Those concerns just make good sense. Packages at best are unwieldy. They're often heavy and stuffed with all kinds of breakable materials. Throw in a purse or a briefcase, a wad of keys way down in a pocket, perhaps a kid or two and you can see why the customer believes closer is better. Regardless of the fact that there may be hundreds of open spaces a quarter mile from your store, if you don't have adequate parking within that magic 150 – 250 feet, you may as well not have parking at all.

Consider also the way the parking lanes and stalls are designed. Some owners have a false belief that by reducing the size of parking spaces they can attract more customers because they'll have more parking. That's really false economy. *Convenient parking* is what the customer wants. That means close to the store, but it also means easy entrance and exit to and from the slot. Generally, parking spaces should be about 20 feet long and 9 feet wide. Double lines between the spaces that allow easy access to the vehicle *with an armload of packages* are desirable. Again, thinking in terms of your customer's real needs is the best way to increase your own bank account.

Packing more spaces into a lot doesn't guarantee more customers just because you can advertise "more" parking. If pulling into those spaces becomes a chore, customers will opt for a lot (and another store/center) where things are more convenient. As this book is being written, large SUVs are a very popular means of transportation for a large segment of the shopping population. They take up a lot of space within a standard parking area. It's always in your best interest to make sure your customers, once they're in the parking space, can actually get out of their vehicle to continue the shopping experience.

Local Economy

Look carefully at the community surrounding any retail store or shopping center you're considering for investment. Is that community's economic base supporting the facility now? If not, why? If so, will it be able to continue that support in the future? A great store in a declining neighborhood may not do great business for very long. What is and what will be the real buying power of the neighborhood? Population count alone isn't enough. An upscale shop featuring high-end tuxedo sales and rentals is not going to do a lot of business in a lower class neighborhood where people need coveralls, work clothing, and steel-toed boots. The needs of the people and the economy just won't support it. A small grocery store, clothing store, hardware store, and other stores serving the real needs of the community could do quite well in the same location. People who wouldn't spend a dime on a tux will spend a small fortune on food, clothing and light bulbs.

Pay special attention to which way the population wind is blowing. For example, if an older population base is selling out to make room for younger families, you will see a radical shift in retail shopping needs. Senior City and Leisure World aren't going to attract a lot of people who need a Toys 'R Us.

You can refer to a large number of tables and charts in business management books that will give you a general feel for the numbers of people needed to support any given business. A trip to your local library or book store will lead you to them. For example, let's say you want to invest in a small, strip shopping center. The charts indicate that such a business needs a population base of 25,000 people. If the neighborhood you're researching has a population base of only 15,000 people, you have your answer. This is a bad location because there just aren't enough customers nearby to keep it going. If the population base is, say, 35,000 you still may not be in a good position. What if there's another shopping center already up and running? Can the market support two centers? If not, can you be competitive enough to survive the economic battle that will follow your grand opening? What are your odds of coming out on top? What services or products can your business offer that the competition cannot?

Competitive Situation

As an investor you have to consider the competitive situation for yourself and also for your tenants. It's important that each of you is successful in your selected location. A good landlord takes care of good tenants. Business attracts more business and the better everyone does, the better everyone's profit picture becomes.

- What is the competition?
- Where is the competition? Do they have a better, more convenient location?
- How close are they to your proposed operation?
- Are they in a strong position? Growing? Declining? Rejuvenating?
- Will they draw customers from you or can you both exist in the same market?
- Can you (and your tenants) be competitive? Can you remain competitive?
- How aggressive is their marketing program? Can you match or beat it?

- What is their reputation in the community?

- How can you combat their strengths and exploit their weaknesses?

- Are you prepared to do battle for market supremacy?

- How prepared are your tenants for real-world marketing and promotion?

Retail outlets can become fantastic real estate investments, provided the buyer does his (or her) homework, plans the acquisition carefully, executes a detailed plan, and has an equally carefully-prepared and executed course of action after the contract is signed.

Buying retail real estate is a great opportunity for one basic reason – people love to buy retail.

Chapter Eighteen

Industrial Real Estate

This category covers a lot of territory: light to heavy manufacturing, assembly plants, manufacturing/office complexes, industrial parks, research and development facilities, processing plants, raw materials storage, and hundreds of other uses related to the production of an uncountable number of products. Industrial properties are remarkably varied and often complex undertakings. You could easily find yourself, and your investment, involved in environmental impacts, safety procedures for exotic raw materials, or new products that have scientists, ethicists and government representatives going, "Well, we never thought about *that* before." Industrial sites also tend to be occupied by long-term tenants, a definite plus for the real estate investor. After all, it costs a lot more to move an industrial furnace or an entire production line than it does to pay a modest yearly increase in rent. That's one reason why in some parts of the country several generations of families have been able to get work "down at the mill."

The bottom line is that if you're interested in the arena of industrial real estate, you have a lot of interesting and profitable opportunities from which to choose. Here's a short list just to give you an idea of the breadth of this category of real estate: light to heavy manufacturing, mining operations, milling, metal fabrication, assembly plants, steel mills and iron works, sawmills, lumber and wood products manufacturing, automobile garages, freight yards, loading and unloading docks, multi-use complexes and industrial parks, energy production, petrochemicals, electronics, and thousands of others. If you really believe that variety is the spice of life, then industrial real estate might just be to your taste. Let's look at some of the challenges and opportunities you'll most likely face.

You'll recognize a few right off the bat.

Location: This one should come as no surprise. Location is important for different reasons to different companies. Some will need to be close to raw materials. For example, a lot of sawmills and lumber manufacturing plants are found right in the middle of the nation's forests. Refineries are often near the centers of oil and gas production. Other industries need to be near their customers or to reliable means of transport to their customers. Rail lines, convenient traffic arteries, rivers and waterways, and airports are major considerations if not necessities. Some have highly specialized needs. For example, there's a major aircraft assembly plant not too far from where I live. One of their essential requirements is an uncluttered air corridor to the wide open spaces for flight testing their craft.

Available labor force: Even in this computerized "push button" world, industry will always need someone to push those buttons. In the past, industry focused its primary hiring efforts on cheap labor for jobs requiring little if any education. People in many communities used to wake up knowing that regardless of education or job skills, they could most likely get a decent job at the local plant. There was always plenty of work, even for the unskilled and uneducated. That's changing in the United States. Those jobs are moving to other nations where labor is inexpensive. American industry today needs a highly skilled labor force. Education, job skills, and an ability to adapt to the dictates of a rapidly changing global market are essential these days.

For the investor looking for good properties, a large population of available labor isn't necessarily a plus factor unless it's the *right* population for industry's needs.

Utilities: Industrial facilities, even clean manufacturing plants, require a lot of electricity, gas, water and other related services. It's a good idea to carefully research the needs of any industrial property you're considering for investment. For example, a lot of plywood and particleboard manufacturing plants use a lot of energy. *But* they also create a lot of waste products such as wood trim and end cuts which can be burned to create their own energy. Some modern plants are practically self-sufficient in some production areas when it comes to fuel. If energy supplies are a problem in your area, they still might not be a problem for a given industry. Don't assume. Investigate and only then make your decision.

Quality of life: The educated and highly skilled workforce needed to meet the nation's industrial needs has one advantage its predecessors never really had: options. They can, for the most part, pick up and go. We're a mobile nation and it's very easy to get from one part of the country to another, from one opportunity (or lack thereof) to better circumstances. Industry has had to come to grips with the non-employment needs of its employees so as to retain those employees. Quality of life is something wise investors factor into their financial equations. If I invest in this facility, are there enough positive features here to assure that the work force will remain and the facility will be able to operate?

A smart investor is concerned with such far ranging factors as good schools for the kids, adult education, museums and galleries, outlets for hobbies and crafts, parks, libraries, shopping, urban recreational outlets, and outdoor recreational opportunities such as lakes, forests and jogging or bicycle trails. Security is another factor. Are the schools and playgrounds safe? What is the crime rate? How serious is the drug problem? Does local law enforcement have a handle on things?

Transportation: Yes, we all live in a world that's wired to the Internet. We can communicate and instantaneously conduct business with South America, Scotland or Shanghai. Still, industry needs an efficient means of getting raw materials to the plant and finished products out to distribution centers, sales outlets, and customers. Good roads are usually essential. Rail, air freight, and water shipment may also be required. Often municipalities, counties or industrial developers invest in transportation and other infrastructure "on their own nickel" just to attract industry. They believe the long-term payoff justifies the upfront expense.

Materials shipment is just one factor. The workforce needs to have reliable transportation so that they can show up for work. In some areas this might mean a good county road system. Other areas might require a mass transportation.

Politics: Depending upon the size and scope of the industries you're evaluating for investment, you might find yourself embroiled in local, state, regional, national or even international politics. Regardless of size and scope, you will be involved in some politics. Taxes and regulations are obvious areas of concern. You might also face challenges related to environmental concerns, land use, population control, and quality of life issues. The same facility might be held up as a pillar of the economic community by one group and as an example of the evils of capitalism run rampant by another. Politics can have a positive or negative affect on the success of an enterprise. If you invest in industrial real estate you can be assured that you will be investing at least some of your time in politics.

Change: Some years ago the effects of change on industry were slow in coming, slow in being used, and slow to evolve into other changes. Owners, investors and industrial designers could create a plant or facility and know that the same basic design would be in use for generations. Today, rapid change is a fact of life. Technology reshapes entire industries seemingly overnight. An expensive production facility designed for one purpose could become obsolete during that same period. The property could lose its usefulness and value just as quickly.

That's an exciting fact really and in the long run change means great opportunity for a great number of people. But if you're considering investing in a building or facility that incorporates a design for special uses, think to the future. Will there be a need for that property tomorrow or are you just investing in what will soon become another empty building in the rust belt? Generally speaking, it's a good idea to invest in properties that are adaptable to many uses rather than to tie yourself (and your funds) down to a single-use facility that could quickly become an industrial "money pit."

One of the real advantages of industrial property is the fact that tenants tend to settle in for long periods of time. It's just too costly to pick up an entire manufacturing facility and move it across the town, the country or the nearest ocean. Of course, there's a down side. Once a facility does make such a move, the vacant property could then remain vacant for an equally long period of time. That makes sense. The building was used, and perhaps even designed for a specific purpose. Once that purpose has moved on, other industries might not be able to easily adapt their operations to the old layout.

Financing: Compared to other real estate financing, getting money for industrial sites or facilities is generally much tougher. That's not to say it can't be done. It can. It's just that bankers and lenders know everything that you've just read. They know all about changing technology, limited use buildings, and long vacancies. They can be tough on a real estate investor and with good reason. The man, woman, or group wanting to borrow money for industrial investment just has to be tougher. The process will be more demanding than applying for money to finance an apartment complex or strip shopping center. Harness all your facts. Know the answers to all the questions before they're asked. Assemble a masterful plan with complete documentation. Cross all the Ts and dot all the Is and then get the financing you need and deserve.

Another factor you'll need to consider is the credit-worthiness of your tenant(s). A long-term lease with terrific terms is still worthless if the tenant is worthless. It's basic business practice to check out the credit rating of someone renting a one-bedroom apartment. Imagine how much more important such checks are on someone renting an entire production facility. Hold out for long-term tenants with solid credit and in a stable industry. And always keep an eye to the future. There were a lot of stable, well-financed buggy whip companies around when Henry Ford started cranking out automobiles. You'll want to rent to the man or woman with vision…and a future. After all, it's your future, too.

Chapter Nineteen

Mobile Home Parks

I'm including a chapter on mobile home parks because they represent a real opportunity and because they're an often-misunderstood opportunity. When mobile homes were first becoming popular, they were mostly purchased by people who were literally on the move and/or who couldn't afford a more expensive standard and immobile starter home. They and the folks who owned them were often the butt of jokes.

That's all changed now. Today the owners of so-called mobile homes represent a far broader spectrum of the American people – and a profitable one for the wise investors who wants to serve the needs of that market and profit by that service. For one thing, mobile homes are very rarely mobile these days. The dwellings can be quite substantial and of considerable size and comfort. In a bit of marketing genius, the industry renamed itself many years ago. Now they produce not mobile homes, but "manu-factured housing." In one stroke they removed a pretty severe image problem and opened up entire new markets of people who would never consider living in a "mobile home."

A Broad and Growing Market

They're very popular with working people, especially those just starting out, because they're relatively inexpensive, can be purchased in a variety of sizes, don't require large lots or acreage, and can be placed just about anywhere.

Seniors and retirees like them for the same reasons. A lot of retirees live in them because they're on a fixed income and manufactured housing is an affordable option. Also, they can have the benefits of a yard, albeit a small one, without having to be concerned with the upkeep of a full-sized lawn.

Arizona, Florida, Nevada and Texas have a lot of upscale seniors living part time in manufactured housing. These folks, while not members of the super rich, are wealthy enough to own two homes. They live up north during the warm months and then move south when the winds, rains and snows show up on their doorstep. They don't live in a mobile home because the *have to.* They make that choice because they *want to.*

Because mobile homes are so compact and require a minimum of "yard" at best, a lot of them can be packed comfortably into a relatively small area. Hence, we get the mobile home park. Some look at these collections of humanity and compare them to sardines in a can. Perhaps, but most mobile home park dwellers see it another way. They see and experience a very real sense of community – even those who live in that community only four to six months a year. Often the first days of the season are like old home week when all these seniors arrive back at their winter base. They don't see themselves as being packed in. Rather, they're close to a bunch of old friends.

The market for mobile home parks is a growing one and I don't see that trend changing in the foreseeable future. Young people always need affordable housing when they're just starting out. Every year science, health, and medicine extend the lives and the quality of lifestyle of our aging population. Instead of moving into the old folks home, these days seniors are maintaining their independence and living good lives close to friends and neighbors. Mobile home parks are an increasingly important element of that lifestyle.

An Efficient Use of Resource

There are a lot of people who do not live in manu-factured housing, and who probably never will, but who are among its biggest boosters. These include environmentalists, city planners, and business people who have the foresight to realize an important fact: mobile home parks are an extremely efficient use of available space. One of the reasons real estate can be so pricey is because "they're not making any more of it." Manufactured housing allows a lot of people to be put into a relatively small area of land. That makes good sense from a variety of viewpoints: land use, tax base, convenience, proximity to goods and services, environmental quality, a sense of community, and as an economic boost to the community at large. Here in Arizona, many of our cities experience tremendous growth equal to that of an entire large town for four to six months of the year. Hundreds of thousands of "snowbirds" arrive every winter. Imagine what kind of positive impact that has on a community.

Of course, as an owner of or investor in a mobile home park you have to cover your bases. The unit(s) must be profitable for the entire year. There must be (1) enough year-round rental units to cover your expenses and earn a profit or (2) the profits from the "snowbird" season must be high enough to justify the expense of the lower-profit summer months. Many investors find a combination the best approach. They have a list of year-round clients, but leave room for the winter guests. Others cater exclusively to full-time, full-year retirees. Any of the options or any combination can be very satisfactory for the investors.

The "sardine can" analogy works only if you think that way and for most manufactured housing dwellers, the proximity of neighbors is a blessing, not a curse. That's especially true if you're aging and perhaps have a few health concerns and wouldn't mind your friends nearby to check in on how you're doing.

Mobile home parks can be established in virtually any setting. I've seen them in rural areas, on the outskirts of towns, in the suburbs and even in downtown areas. In many cities entire neighborhoods or substantial portions of neighborhoods are made up of mobile home parks.

Savvy real estate investors love mobile home parks for all these reasons and more. Managed properly, they provide an excellent return for many years.

Follow the Basic Rules

I find it helpful to think of buying and managing mobile home parks in much the same way I think about buying and managing apartment buildings. Your approach is almost identical. In fact, you might want to refer back to Chapter 15 and mentally substitute "mobile home park" for "apartment." Here's a summary of the key points.

Follow the "one-hour rule." Look for property that is within an hour's drive of your home or office. A half hour's drive is even better. You'll need to be close to your investment when things go wrong. And believe me, some time some thing will go wrong and you'll need to be on the scene as quickly as possible. This remains true even if you have an on-site manager and a full-time maintenance man or maintenance crew.

Conduct serious research before making your purchase. Consider the city, town or community and the environment you want. Then go looking. Read the classified ads. Drive around and note the "for sale" yard signs. Make inquiries and talk to the owners. Talk to current tenants and people in the neighborhood. Get facts and impressions from people in the business and people in the know. Invest serious time looking. There are innumerable investment opportunities for you. The first one you come across may or may not be the "magic" one. Invest enough time to be certain before you start writing checks.

Remember the big three keys to success in real estate: employment, recreation and transportation. Employment can be an important factor even to retirees. Many seniors continue working at a variety of jobs after their official retirement. Some have to. Some merely want to keep on being productive in the job market. And some just like to be out and about and around a lot of people. Obviously, jobs are a major factor if your client base will consist primarily of working-age people.

Recreation is important to everyone. Manufactured housing is generally small. That's often one of the real attractions to making that purchase in the first place. But being small they may not be conducive to entertaining a lot of relatives or friends. Nearby recreational outlets become a necessity. Additionally, recreation is an important element of living the good life – whether you're just starting out or nearing the end of the trail. Again, consider your primary market and make sure the nearby recreational outlets match the needs and desires of your customer base.

Even in an automobile-driven society, other transportation outlets are important. People need access to major traffic arteries to get to their place of employment or to all those nearby recreational outlets. People who no longer can or who choose to no longer drive need a convenient city bus system or some type of senior-care mobility.

Know What You're Buying

Don't be intimidated by the size of the space available. You can probably manage a lot more customers than you believe. There are economies in size and the more clients you serve the easier it becomes to spread the costs of maintenance and repair around.

Know what you're buying. Evaluate the neighborhood and the community. Is the area new and developing, growing and maturing, in decline, or is it bouncing back from a decline and in the rejuvenation phase? Opportunities can be found in all four stages, but make sure your plans match the growth pattern of your chosen area.

Be sure to "crunch the numbers" to be as certain as is possible that you can earn a profit from your mobile home park. Examine every detail very carefully. Don't blindly accept the assurances of the present owner. Look at the books to get an accurate and long-term appraisal of the financial situation. He or she may quite naturally put things in a light that is, shall we say, more favorable than they might actually be. Remember, it's your responsibility to be a responsible buyer. Ask questions. Take notes. Check and double check the facts. Only then consider making your move.

Your rental spaces and/or units have to be competitive with market rates. There are taxes to consider, insurance rates, maintenance, upkeep, repair, and management costs. Prices on everything are sure to rise. Consider the cost of borrowing money, city maintenance fees, utilities, inspections, computers and computer programs, telephones, pencils and paper, filing cabinets, coffee, coffee makers, coffee filters, paper napkins to clean up coffee spills and so on and so on. It never stops. Factor everything into your equations. As always, it's a good policy to hope for the best but to base your plans on handling the worst that could possibly happen.

Whenever armies march into war they have a plan for successfully marching out of that conflict – at least the successful armies approach the situation that way. It's called an exit strategy. Develop your own exit strategy or at least the rudiments of one should you ever desire or need to sell your property. You'll probably want to hold onto a successful enterprise, but you can never predict the future. Fortune or misfortune may send your career on an unexpected path. It's a good idea to have a list of options available should that time ever arrive.

The important thing for investors to consider when it comes to mobile home parks is - *to consider investing in mobile home parks.* The mobile home industry has taken a lot of bad raps over the decades and most of them were unjustified. That's why the term manufactured housing was invented and why it caught on so fast and so well. Mobile home park ownership and management isn't for everybody, but the investment can work out very well for many individuals and groups. And because it's an investment area that doesn't come immediately to mind for a lot of folks, there are often better than average deals for the savvy investor. It's an area worth a good look.

Chapter Twenty

Trust Deeds for Fantastic Income

A trust deed is a legal document in which the legal and equitable title of a piece of property is transferred to a specific trustee(s) as security for a loan on a piece of property. Three participants are involved. The *Investor* (or lender), the *Trustor* (the borrower) and the *Trustee,* an impartial third party who (1) holds and administers the funds and (2) acts for the investors. Sounds pretty basic, doesn't it? And it is. Trust deeds also offer you a fantastic opportunity to earn real wealth through real estate.

Here's how it works. A borrower and a lender create a loan which is secured by a piece of real property. Title to this property is then transferred to the trustee. During the time of the loan the trustor has the right of possession of the property and the right to use, encumber or even sell it. Other stipulations agreed on by lender and borrower may of course be placed within the agreement. The trustee, who has the power of sale, holds the title until all elements stipulated in the loan agreement are met. The power of sale held by the trustee is important. Should the trustor default on the loan, he or she then has the power to sell the property to a new owner. If there's no default and the trustor fulfils the obligations of the loan, the property is then re-conveyed to the original owner and the loan or lien is removed.

The concept of a trust deed isn't some new financial angle. It's been around for a long time and is therefore a proven way of earning a high return on an investment. They are to my mind a safe and secure means of building and maintaining financial well being and can provide a road to great wealth. Even investors with widely diverse financial interests, should at least give some thought to adding this element to their portfolio.

There are two very real advantages for the investor. One, the rate of return is much better than you can get from such traditionally safe investments as bank certificates of deposits or money markets. In today's economy those and similar vehicles are little better than parking your money. Two, investors don't have to ride the wild up and down swings of the rollercoaster known as the stock market. Trust deeds offer investors a much more tranquil ride.

Advantages of Investing in Trust Deeds

There are many. Here is a brief summary of what I consider the top reasons for considering trust deeds as elements in your own portfolio.

Security. This is at or near the top of the list for all investors. It's hard to get more secure than a trust deed because the loan is secured by real property, either undeveloped land, developed properties, buildings, homes or other solid real estate. To borrow an old advertising phrase from the phone company, you can actually "reach out and touch" your security. Unless you've made the mistake of making a loan against some obviously bad property, it's very difficult to avoid making a profit.

Excellent returns. Investors earn higher rates than through many other vehicles. There's a very good reason. Individual investors (lenders) are as a rule much more flexible than banks, savings and loans, or other financial institutions. They're not nearly as hemmed in by local, state and federal regulation. All this flexibility translates directly into a higher rate of return. As with all successful arrangements, everybody gives something so that everybody gets something – especially the investor.

Speed. The entire process is (or at least can be) a lot faster and smoother than a traditional loan. Lender/investors don't have to be concerned with the process of going through a loan committee or with other steps that can slow down the progress of setting up the trust deed. This is attractive to the borrowers who want the most flexible and beneficial terms they can possibly get. Generally, the private lenders can make decisions swiftly and move fast once a decision is made. That's a benefit to both sides of the agreement.

Reduced risk. The people borrowing the money are, as a rule, much better risks than the "average Joe" walking in off the street who struts up to the loan officer and asks "'ya got any money?" These borrowers are people with existing money and assets. Perhaps they're in a temporary bind or have access to an unexpected opportunity and need a sudden influx of cash. Whatever, the lender isn't betting on an unknown. Again, you can look at, walk up to, touch and tour the real estate asset securing the loan.

Good LTV. The initials refer to Loan-To-Value ratio. What is the value of the loan against the value of the security for that loan? In most trust deeds the value of the real property is more than the value of the loan. They offer an excellent LTV and are therefore considered very good loans.

Nonjudicial foreclosure. That's a fancy way of saying your financial tush is covered. The security for the loan is real property. Should the borrower default on the loan, the process of nonjudicial foreclosure gives you the right to sell the property to recoup your money. That "nonjudicial" part is important. It means you, the lender, don't have to go through the tedious and time-consuming process of a court proceeding. You just foreclose on your own – no lawyers, no judges, no courtroom theatrics. Regulations vary, but some states permit the lender to initiate the process the first day after a loan payment is missed. This is a case where the rules are actually set up in favor of the lender.

No right of redemption. The legal phrase "right of redemption" means that a borrower has the right to repurchase his or her interest in the real estate property securing the loan after the judicial foreclosure sale. You'll find this clause in most mortgages. It's not a part of most trust deeds and that's to your advantage. If you engage in a nonjudicial foreclosure sale of the securing property, that sale is final – no ifs, ands or buts. It's over. End of story. This feature is important to the lender because title to the property can be handed over to the new owner right away. Again, speed is a real benefit associated with trust deeds.

You probably won't have to endure these problems. As I just noted, most borrowers involved in trust deeds are pretty good risks. Still, it's good to know that the options to protect your investment are there should you ever need them.

You'll discover other rather significant benefits, too. Here's a list of the most attractive features.

- Liquidity. Trust deeds are very easy to buy and sell and you can even trade them.
- They pay a high interest rate. Generally, it's a rate much higher than you can earn through your friendly neighborhood bank.
- Interest payments generate monthly income.
- Because trust deeds usually come with a full-payment clause in the event they are sold, few trust deeds ever make it to full term.
- Trust deeds can provide the security for a loan.
- The lender does not have responsibility to maintain or repair the property. Those hassles and expenses remain with the borrower because the loan amount is being amortized, the investor's protection increases month-by-month.
- The full face value of the deed is shown on the financial statement, even on a discounted trust deed.
- Investors pay taxes only on received interest, thus reducing tax liability.
- Generally, most property increases in value. Equity builds up over time. Therefore the investor's investment becomes more valuable year after year.

You don't hear a lot about trust deeds as investments. I suspect many people who could take advantage of this remarkable opportunity have never even heard about it. Perhaps this chapter will in some way make up for that oversight. Trust deeds really do provide investors with a fantastic opportunity to earn and protect wealth. Whether you choose this route or not is, of course, up to you, but I hope you will at least explore this safe, secure and financially rewarding option.

Chapter Twenty-one

State Tax Certificates

Here's another lucrative area of investment often overlooked or even unknown by most investors. They're called state tax certificates and here's what they're all about. Property owners sometimes get into financial straits. The why and wherefore aren't important here, but for some reason the owners become unable to pay their property taxes. Some people just plain forget to do so. But the state (or county) has its own bills to pay. The public demands its public services. Therefore, the government puts a lien on that property and then sells tax certificates, also called tax liens, to make up for lost tax revenue.

You and I can buy those certificates and I highly recommend that you take a close look at this little-known opportunity. Not only does the buyer acquire the right to collect those taxes, he (or she) can also collect interest on them. When you buy one of these certificates you also acquire the right to: foreclose on the property if the taxes are not paid; evict the tenants under certain conditions; and you also get the right to dispose of the property as you see fit.

The rate of return can be very high. For example, investors purchasing tax certificates "over the counter" (not sold at public auction) earn a flat-rate of 18 percent for the first year. I think you'll agree that it's hard to top that kind of rate regardless of the investment vehicle you choose. The various states set their own rates, so before investing check locally to find the applicable conditions in your area.

Here's an important factor in your favor. These interest rates are set by state law. They're not affected by upswings or downswings in the economy, changes in administrations, wars, pestilence, global warming, or whatever scam the boys on Wall Street have in mind for the day. They can only be changed by an act of the state government. How much more secure or stable can an interest rate be?

How to Buy Tax Certificates

The process, with state-by-state variations, is pretty basic. A property owner can no longer pay property taxes. The state (or county or municipality) steps in and holds a public auction. The amount owed may include more than just the taxes. For example, also included may be back taxes, interest, penalties, legal fees, court costs, and administrative fees. The amount owed, called the accounts receivable, is sold in the form of tax certificates or liens. In many states you are not required to be a resident. You might be able to make your bid by mail or even online.

Investors bid on the accounts receivable just as bidders would make offers for fine art, jewelry, cattle and horses, real property, or any thing offered in an auction. Being the highest bidder and acquiring the receivables doesn't automatically make the investor a property owner, although that can happen. Only the amount owed is purchased, not the property itself. However, if the owner doesn't make his or her payments, the investor can instigate foreclosure proceedings and acquire the property. When this happens, and it happens frequently, the investors become a property owner at a fantastically low price.

If you're interested in purchasing tax certificates, don't focus on the property ownership aspect of this opportunity. After all, the original owner might be able to make those payments. In reality, acquiring the property for just the taxes is a matter that's not in your control. Focus instead on the fantastic financial return you'll earn. Tax certificates can be great investments in and of themselves. If by the way you happen to become a property owner, consider it icing on the cake.

As with any auction, it's wise to keep firm control of your emotions. It's easy to get caught up in a buying "frenzy" and overbid. Make sure that you don't pay more for the tax certificate than the property is worth.

A Fast Return on Your Investment

One of the real benefits of owning tax certificates is the fact that you start earning interest immediately. There's no delay or time lag at all. Provided the investor does his homework and doesn't buy a lien that costs more than the property, he or she practically can't lose. The investor is owed the amount of the lien plus significant interest on that lien and there's always the possibility of acquiring a nice piece of property for a song. I have read of a case where a multi-millionaire's business managers made a basic mistake in bookkeeping that caused the man to miss paying something just under $50,000 in taxes on one of his multi-million dollar homes. Mistakes are mistakes and he paid dearly for that one. The home was sold for taxes. That's right. Some sharp-eyed investor picked up a piece of property valued in the millions for less than fifty grand. Incredible opportunities like that don't come along every day, but very real and significant opportunities do come along every day.

Here's another matter to consider. Every man's loss is another man's gain. That's not a cruel or callous comment. It's just the way things are. When the economy goes south, people get in financial binds. Those binds are also opportunities for people buying state tax certificates. It just stands to reason. Times get tough. Profits dwindle. Jobs are cut back. Companies downsize. And people sometimes can't pay the taxes on their properties. That person's loss can be your gain. And that's just the way things work.

Is There a Downside?

Of course. There's a downside to everything. Your beautiful new baby will start crying at 2 a.m. That wonderful, new SUV will at some time blow a tire. The additional responsibilities attached to your promotion and raise in pay will increase your stress levels. And if you don't do your homework and plan your investments carefully, you could lose money in real estate.

Make sure that you can afford to "tote the note" when you buy a tax certificate. Add up all the real costs, the probable costs, and even the remotely possible costs. Make sure that you can afford those expenses for the duration of your investment.

I think it essential that you personally inspect or at least hire a qualified inspector to look at the property in question before you purchase the tax certificate. Yes, I know I've said that you're not buying the property, you're buying the lien. Still, everything is based upon that property. Don't you think it's worth a little look-see? Suppose you make the investment, the owner can't make the payments, and you end up with the property only to find that your "windfall" is located in a floodplain or earthquake zone?

As with most investments, you can avoid virtually every downside if you will conduct enough serious research, develop an intelligent investment plan, and implement that plan carefully and with awareness of the changing market. Sure, there's work involved, a lot of it, but the payoff is well worth the effort.

Where to Invest?

By now you really shouldn't have to ask. Remember the title of this book. Arizona, Florida, Nevada, and Texas are four of the best states in which to purchase state tax certificates. For example, Texas offers an interest rate of 25 percent and Florida offers 18 percent. Where else can you get those kinds of returns?

Chapter Twenty-Two

Final Thoughts

The bubble has burst. People are at last realizing that the stock market and mutual funds are no longer a safe place for financial investment. Sure, there have been good times to own stocks and even 2003 has seen a nice rebound. Unfortunately, the bottom line is that the vast majority of investors still have less money today in stocks and mutual funds than they had four or more years ago. The bloodbath of 2000, 2001, and 2002 was experienced by 80 million Americans who lost 50 to 80 percent of their life savings. Like the song *Dixie* says, "old times there are not forgotten." If I might be forgiven for passing along a bit of poetic advice, "Look away. Look away."

Nobody, and I really mean nobody, should ever forget that owning stocks and mutual funds means taking a huge risk with your money. Millions of people cannot afford to take those risks. Believe me, many who did are living with profound regret today. Anyone who is within ten to fifteen years of retiring and cannot afford risk is especially vulnerable. People in that category should avoid the market like the plague. As I've repeatedly said, if you really like to invest in stocks because you like the challenge, enjoy the volatility, and hope for significant returns, go right ahead. But please be careful. Limit your exposure to five to fifteen percent of your total net worth. Invest only in stocks. Stay completely away from mutual funds. Perhaps you'll be successful and will buy and sell the right stocks. It can happen.

I heed my own advice. I'm invested in the stock market, but I don't exceed my limit, which is 15 percent of my net worth. If a major downturn occurs, and it will, I might be bruised, but I won't be battered or ruined. If I watch things develop carefully, I might even be smart enough to sell out before the bottom drops out.

Expertise and experience isn't enough to guarantee success. I've been studying the stock market and mutual funds for more than four decades, yet I have owned several stocks that have been pounded unmercifully or that have completely gone under. I took major hits during 2000 - 2001 on Worldcom, Global Crossing, Lucent Technology, Gateway, Nortel Networks, and Broadcom. I'm not proud to discuss my misfortune, but there's a point to be made. I was not ruined or badly hurt financially because the losses represented only a small percentage of my investment portfolio.

Sadly, many of my clients and associates did not heed that advice and have seen their fortunes devastated. Several retired clients have been forced to re-enter the work place even though they are in their seventies. A lot of retirees are spending their golden years working under the "golden arches" these days. Many clients can't afford luxuries such as vacations, new cars, or even an expensive night on the town. Some of them will never have those kinds of experiences again.

I started writing *Be Money Smart in Investments, Real Estate, and Insurance* in 1999. In those pages I repeatedly warned investors that stocks and mutual funds were extremely risky after the bull market that roared through the 1990s. I urged investors to lighten their portfolio – drastically. Unfortunately, many of my clients were so certain that they were going to make a fortune in the market they refused to take my advice. Many of them read my book and even acknowledged my concerns, but their greed had overtaken their logic. They ignored the warning signs and kept their money in stocks and mutual funds.

Now that the market crash has hit, taken its toll and is an accepted reality, I've seen a remarkable change in virtually every client. The realities of the marketplace have finally made them listen to common sense. Having seen their friends and associates hammered by the market, or having been hammered themselves, most of my clients have sold 100 percent of their stocks and mutual funds. Others have at least dramatically reduced the amount of their investment. That's good because the problems with the stock market, especially mutual funds, are just beginning to reach the public.

Recently New York Attorney General Eliot Spitzer uncovered a series of mutual fund scandals. I've written about that sad, but necessary event in this book. Now, that the information is coming out look for mutual fund redemptions to hit record numbers. This is hard for many to fathom, but mutual fund giant Putnam experienced a withdrawal of $4.4 *billion* in one week in November, 2003. One week! And that's billion with a big, expensive B. Additionally, the company has been ravaged by more than $4 billion redeemed by institutional investors including state pension plans in Vermont, Rhode Island, Iowa and Pennsylvania. That totals to more than $8 billion withdrawn from Putnam in a remarkably short period of time. That enormous figure is greater than the total assets in thousands of other mutual funds. These scandals are the biggest to hit the market since The Great Depression. Some of the very top names in the industry are involved. These include Putnam, Janus, Strong, Bank of America, Prudential, Alger Alliance, and Bank One. I wonder just how much bleaker the situation can become for the nation's mutual funds industry.

Not too long ago mutual funds were the darlings of Wall Street. Assets were in the trillions of dollars. Things are different today and I can't say this with enough emphasis: *withdraw your money from mutual funds now.* If you must invest in the stock market, conduct some very serious research and place your money in quality stocks. Just make sure that your total investment in the market does not exceed five to fifteen percent of your total net worth.

More and more people are beginning to realize the value of investing in real estate. Stocks and mutual fund investing has cost individuals and families uncounted amounts of money. Many will never recover. Banks and S&Ls and money market accounts have been paying meager returns for several years in a row. I'm writing this on November 7 2003. I've just looked at the CD rates posted in *USA Today* and it is hard for me to believe how abysmally low they have fallen. For example, a five-year CD provides a paltry 3.04 percent and a 2 ½ year CD offers only a rate of 1.75 percent. From an investor's point of view that's just pathetic.

From my perspective things are pretty basic. Stocks and mutual funds during the past 3 ½ years have reduced the value of most investors' money by 50 percent or more. If you have been keeping your money in the so-called safe places, such as banks, S&Ls or money market accounts, you have been rewarded with nothing more than lousy returns. Rates have averaged from ½ percent to about three percent annually. As I said – pathetic.

Well, if you haven't already done so, it's time to take immediate action. Start looking and evaluating real estate now. You want to develop a plan so that you will have about 75 percent of your total net worth in real estate investments. That's the goal for people who want financial stability, security, and who want to earn terrific returns on their investments.

Here's a word of caution. Don't dash out and start buying up real estate without a plan. Take your time and carefully evaluate the most intelligent way to diversify your money into a portfolio of numerous real estate investments. Please realize that not all real estate deals represent a good deal. And good real estate doesn't automatically mean a good deal for some investors. It's important to develop clear goals, realistic benchmarks, to understand the process, and to have a grasp on your financial capabilities over time before making any decisions. For income safety you can't find anything better than 1st or 2nd mortgages (Deeds of Trust), state tax certificates, and discount mortgages. Again, evaluate which options are best for your individual situation. Find knowledgeable, trustworthy and accessible people who can provide the advice and expertise you'll need, especially in your early days of investing.

After you have selected the best place to invest for your income needs, you will want to consider numerous real estate investments that offer growth, appreciation, and tax savings. Currently, numerous high quality, income real estate investments are yielding eight to ten percent returns. Some are doing better than that. There is a wide range of real estate available and you can tailor your selections to meet your personal needs and comfort level. Personally, my number one choice is raw land investment in the four booming states of Arizona, Florida, Nevada and Texas and this is where I recommend you invest a substantial amount of your available investment money. These states offer tremendous investment opportunities.

Remember, you always want to diversify your holdings based on your total available capital. Raw land is my favorite because the opportunities for substantial gains in these four states is enhanced because they are experiencing significant and sustained population growth. Other options are readily available: houses, condos, town homes, duplexes, multiplexes, office buildings, hotels, shopping centers, mini-warehouses, mobile home parks, industrial buildings and properties, and the list goes on and on and on. As do the profits.

It's high time for investors to realize that real estate is the only sensible, safe, easily accessible, and timely way to invest the majority of their money. Stocks and mutual funds have slipped dramatically and a long list of negatives continues to negatively impact their performance. Economy-draining wars, class action lawsuits, global competition, poor management, dishonest and unscrupulous CEOs and board members who can run a company into the ground are just a few examples of the problems facing the industry. This list could go on for pages, but suffice it to say that the real downside is that you have absolutely no control over your investments when any or any combination of these events hit.

When you honestly evaluate all the factors, real estate has so many advantages over stocks and mutual funds that there really shouldn't be any debate over the matter. Your real estate investment options are virtually unlimited. The price structures are so varied that practically anyone can participate regardless of his or her economic status. They can be as simple or as complex as the needs, education level, financial abilities, interest level or availability of time permit. You can maintain control over your investment. They're imminently logical. They're real. They're safe. They can provide fantastic returns. What else do you want from an investment?

Real estate is the only place to invest the majority of your money. And within that wonderful world of opportunities, you will find no better locations than those offered by the exciting, on-the-move, growing states of Arizona, Florida, Nevada and Texas.

Chapter Twenty-Three

How Do I Start Buying Real Estate?

The short answer, especially if you're new in this business, is *carefully.* A slightly longer and more detailed answer follows. Here is a brief look at five basic steps that will get you started. Of course, you'll want to use the in-depth information found in the preceding chapters. Continue your studies in real estate, too. Consult with professionals in the business. Read other books. Checkout the online resources and subscribe to real estate magazines and newsletters. Do your homework. But implementing a sound plan is the first and most essential step to successful real estate investing. These steps will get you started on the right foot.

Step #1. Look first to the incredible opportunities for investment found in Arizona, Florida, Nevada and Texas. I don't care if you live in Washington, Wisconsin, or West Virginia, geography is no longer a serious impediment to serious and successful real estate investing. You already know from this book just how great these opportunities can be.

Realize that regardless of your street address, you can still take advantage of those opportunities. You can fly across the entire nation in a matter of hours and if you can't fly you can drive on a marvelous, fast and safe interstate highway system. Business, financial, and real estate specific newspapers, magazines, and newsletters can be delivered to your door or even through your computer. The mail still runs and at express speeds if you want. The Internet offers a world of research resources, contacts and opportunities to conduct business in periods of time so short that they would astound business professionals a few years ago.

You're limited only by your imagination. And just imagine what you can accomplish in Arizona, Florida, Nevada and Texas!

Step #2. Select real estate brokers and/or agents to help you achieve your goals. Every one of these four states has very high quality brokers, agents, and companies to assist people in buying and selling real estate. I know this from extensive personal experience. Find, evaluate very carefully, and then choose the right company and person(s) for your needs. Select people with whom you are comfortable and who have a great track record in the business. Ask around, get references and follow up on those references. This choice is extremely important, so take your time. Work with the best and success is sure to follow! Some of the best known companies are: Century 21, ReMax, and for commercial companies C.B. Richard Ellis.

Find the best people and work with them, especially if you are just beginning in real estate. Your agent may work in residential or commercial areas and also will probably be in a position to recommend other professionals in more specialized areas. Remember, these folks make their money on commissions, so they have a real incentive to give you outstanding service. I have known and worked closely with numerous real estate brokers and agents who have done a fantastic job for us in many areas. They and hundreds of other top notch professionals will be pleased to provide you with their real estate background once you have found the person(s) you want on your team. Everything will fall into place very quickly.

Step #3. Please feel free to contact us for a free, no-obligation evaluation of the services we can provide you. We can be reached at the contact points listed in the back of this book. If you prefer to work with someone else, we have real estate contacts in all four states and will be happy to refer you to a company, broker or agent in the state or states of your choice.

Step #4. If you live in a state other than one of the booming four, and if you're really concerned about your ability to conduct successful business out of state, then start at home. You undoubtedly have first-hand knowledge of the primary growth areas and other important factors to weigh before making a real estate purchase. Get your feet wet, get some experience, build up your confidence, and then I urge you to consider just how well you can really do in Arizona, Florida, Nevada and Texas.

Step #5. You certainly can pursue finding real estate properties on your own. There's no law that says you have to work with a broker or agent. That's your decision and you may produce fantastic results by your own efforts. My recommendation, though is to work with professionals in the industry. They have the knowledge, experience, contacts and the motivation to do their level best in helping you achieve your real estate goals. I believe you'll achieve those goals faster and a whole lot easier. The commissions they earn are worth every penny. You'll avoid many of the painful mistakes found in the "school of hard knocks" and, more important, the magnitude and quality of services they provide will prove to be of inestimable value to you.

END

CONTACT US

In the event you have questions, comments, or want to contact us, we can be reached at the following address:

Robert J. Davis
8327 Vista Del Lago
Scottsdale, AZ 85255
Phone: 480-577-9930

Craig A Davis
Phone: 480-330-3296